EVERYDAY PARENTING

Edited by Alex Sibley

Foreword by Dorothy and Paige Patterson

SEMINARY HILL
PRESS

Everyday Parenting
Edited by Alex Sibley
Copyright © 2017 by Seminary Hill Press

Seminary Hill Press (SHP) is the publishing arm of Southwestern Baptist
Theological Seminary, 2001 West Seminary Drive, Fort Worth, Texas 76115.

ISBN-10: 0-9988325-1-0
ISBN-13: 978-0-9988325-1-7

Table of Contents

FOREWORD

By Dorothy and Paige Patterson[1]

Scuba diving with the sharks of Australia's Barrier Reef was a challenge. Shooting the rapids beneath Iguaçu Falls on the border between Brazil and Argentina took my breath away. Surrounded by sixty angry elephants in Zimbabwe, to say the least, was great for the encouragement of prayer. Crossing into communist countries carrying the contraband of the Word of God and wondering how life would be in prison was certainly exciting. Then there was the really scary stuff—serving as the pastor of several Baptist churches and being president of three different seminaries to train ministers. But nothing Dorothy and I ever attempted demanded as much as the task of parenting. We have experienced more profound terror, unnerving decision-making, and genuine crisis counseling in rearing two children and investing in the lives of two grandchildren than in all of our many adventures of life. Of course, this latter endeavor has also garnered the most pleasurable, highly stimulating, and memorable moments of life.

Therefore, Dorothy and I welcome this perceptive and important volume. Everyone wants to ask the Lord some profound question upon arriving in heaven. Ours is simple: "Why, dear Lord, did you not make it possible for us to have children when we were old enough to have at least a distant notion about what to do?"

---

[1]Dorothy and Paige Patterson are the first lady and president, respectively, of Southwestern Baptist Theological Seminary in Fort Worth, Texas.

If we had only possessed this volume, I am confident that we would have made fewer than half the mistakes and that we would have done more than twice as much good with our charges. As a matter of truth, we are sufficiently impressed with this volume to say that any parent who has a desire to rear happy, successful, and Christ-honoring children could do nothing better than invest in a copy of this book and then read it about six times until he begins to think like the authors think.

Of course, we have known the backstories, and these facts enhance the contributions in this anthology. Most of these authors have walked a deep valley as a parent. They have accepted these assignments as an opportunity to show confidence in the providential oversight of our omniscient God. The content of the chapters alone is revolutionary. But written against the backdrop of their own hours of testing and triumph colors the pages in the bright hues of the powerful display of God and the truth that in our weakness is His strength made perfect (2 Corinthians 12:9).

The burden of the years and the blessings of experience have underscored to us a thousand times over the critical nature of the family. The family is the first and, in so many ways, the most important of God's institutions. The city, the polis, the community, and the state all have critical roles in preserving order in the social sphere. The church of the redeemed is the special object of God's affection and is the next to most critical entity for the preservation of order and the teaching of God's principles. But the family is the conduit chosen of God for the responsibility of teaching the next generation the truths of God. The task of exhibiting love, compassion, forgiveness, and justice is laid at the feet of the parent. The assignments of leading little girls into beautiful feminine lives and building little boys into strong men are the mountains that each parent must climb.

The authors of this volume make no apology for their confidence in the Bible as the perfect text for guidance in child rearing. The entire approach of Southwestern Baptist Theological Seminary is that wisdom arises from many points on the compass. Parents are entitled to wisdom wherever it arises and should utilize it all. But to have an accurate compass, one must have a tool that orients itself to the north or the compass will never lead to safety. True north is the Word of God revealed in the Bible. From Evan and Melanie Lenow's chapter on the text-driven nature of child development to Dean Nichols' emphasis on the value of the book of Proverbs in preparing the next generation for changing the social order from the matrix of the home, our readers are pointed to the fact that God has spoken a sure and certain word that we must follow. As evangelicals, we are confident that the Bible is God's Word not only for salvation but also for all of life.

Everyday Parenting is not a book for the faint of heart. You will never climb a higher peak, nor will the Mariana Trench rival the depths to which you will descend in taking the mantle of parenthood. To even begin the journey, you will need to be at your best spiritually, and you will need to have the anointing of God as in no other enterprise of your life. Therefore, we commend to you one of the best books that we ever read. Remember to read it once, and then again and again until you have it in your heart. Make it a resource to which you repeatedly go for biblical solutions to the challenges of this world. We thank God for the contribution of wisdom and experience coming from these authors.

Dorothy and Paige Patterson
Southwestern Baptist Theological Seminary

Introduction

By Alex Sibley

Martha had nearly died giving birth just three weeks prior, so she had to crawl on her hands and knees to the cradle of her infant son, for that was the most she could do. Initially, the cradle had been placed by her bedside, but her family was forced to move it away from her to the middle of the room when they realized she would not cease her attempts to rock the cradle despite being too weak to do so. But on this particular day, the bed-ridden mother found herself alone with the child, and so, declining the interest of her own health, Martha slipped out of bed, crawled to the middle of the room, and looked down at the place where he lay.

Standing on her knees beside the cradle, she used one hand to steady her frail, delicate frame, and the other she used to hold the little hands of her three-week-old baby. Then, with all the strength she had remaining, she voiced a prayer to God.

This was no general prayer of blessing upon her child, though, as her heart's desire for her son was for more than just a blessed life. No, she wanted far more than that for him, and so she prayed with much greater intentionality. Summoning every ounce of faith in her spirit, Martha prayed first of all that God would save her son and, second, that God would call him to preach.

One wonders if Martha imagined at that time the full extent to which this prayer would be answered. Understanding that God is a God who does immeasurably more than all we can ask or even imagine,[2] she would likely admit that she did not. Even so, she surely had high hopes for the boy, so when her expectations were met and, perhaps, then exceeded, she likely rejoiced to a higher degree than most would be able to comprehend. For her son was Lee Rutland Scarborough, and this prayer of his mother was the first step toward his becoming an evangelist, a pastor, one of the founding faculty of Southwestern Baptist Theological Seminary, the first occupant and namesake for the first-ever chair of evangelism in a seminary (Southwestern's "Chair of Fire"), the second president of Southwestern, one-time president of the Southern Baptist Convention, and, in direct answer to his mother's prayer, a preacher of the Gospel of Jesus Christ.[3] Indeed, L.R. Scarborough is among the great figures of modern Baptist history, a most useful instrument in the hands of God during his lifetime, and his story of impacting countless lives for eternity began with this, his mother's prayer.

The significance of Martha's spiritual investment in her child cannot be overstated. Taking her cradle-side prayer to heart, L.R. Scarborough himself later wrote, "Parents should pray that God will call their children and make the home atmosphere favorable for their doing God's will. My mother gave me to the ministry in soulful supplication when I was three weeks of age. Parents can greatly help or hinder God in this matter."[4]

Certainly, Martha Scarborough—as well as her husband George—serves as a good role model for how parents can "help" in the matter of spiritually nourishing their children. Beyond praying this specific prayer, she and George also cultivated within their home an atmosphere conducive to all five of their children becoming followers of Christ (and, indeed, they all did[5]). They

---

[2]"Now to him who is able to do immeasurably more than all we ask or imagine, according to his power that is at work within us..." (Ephesians 3:20, NIV).

[3]Furthermore, when Southwestern later established an undergraduate school, it was named "Scarborough College" in his honor.

[4]Lee R. Scarborough, *Recruits for World Conquests* (New York: Fleming H. Revell Company, 1914), 26.

[5]In total, George and Martha had nine children, but four died in infancy, so

gathered with the children every day around the "family altar" for Scripture reading and worship through song; George, a frontier Baptist preacher, brought his children along whenever he preached revival meetings under brush arbors, in dugouts, and in schoolhouses; and the two even gave up their personal aspirations of building a home for themselves in order to send Lee to college instead.[6] This would prove to be a wise choice, for it was there that Lee surrendered to God's call to preach.

Following his decision, Lee immediately wrote a letter to his parents to inform them of the news. R.T. Hanks, then-pastor of the First Baptist Church of Abilene and family friend of the Scarboroughs, was present when this letter was received. He later recollected:

> Lee never knew the scene in that home when his big hearted father and deeply pious mother received that news. I can never recall it without tears; that blessed mother, brushing away the tears, said: "I am not surprised. I knew it was coming. The Lord promised me that Lee would preach long ago!" Then the noble father said: "Pastor, I know I realize what I say, and I can say it out of a full heart: I had rather my boy would be a preacher of Christ's gospel than President of the United States."[7]

---

the five mentioned here are those who lived to adulthood. Four of the five, including Lee, professed faith in Christ at an early age; the fifth did so as an adult, a few months after their father died. Interestingly, the Gospel invitation to which he finally responded was extended by his youngest brother, Lee, during a revival service.

[6]For a full account of this story, see *The House That Was Never Built: An Excerpt from* Recruits for World Conquests by Charles T. Ball (Fort Worth, TX: Seminary Hill Press).

[7]H.E. Dana, *Lee Rutland Scarborough: A Life of Service* (Nashville, TN: Broadman Press, 1942), 24.

L.R. Scarborough would later reflect highly on his parents' spiritual influence:

> I count as the richest inheritance of my life that which my father and mother left me and the other children in faithful lives of consecration and service to God and humanity. Their consecrated lives, their faithful, loyal service to Christ, to his truth, to his churches, and to his work, their sacrificial toils and economy for me, creating in my heart the desire for an education, their giving me an education, their faith, their prayers, their love, constitute my richest earthly inheritance. They both died triumphant in the gospel, and for these years they have been with Jesus, and I shall some sweet day join them in that bloodwashed throng who with Christ will appear in the heavens at his glorious return.[8]

Imagine having your children say this of you. Imagine having your prayers answered in such a way as Martha Scarborough's were. Imagine receiving from your child a letter indicating that, just as you had prayed, he has surrendered to the call to preach. Imagine your child going on to become a pastor, a preacher, a renowned evangelist, a prolific author, a seminary professor, a seminary president, and president of a national convention. Imagine your child leading countless souls to Christ, expanding the Kingdom of God through an undeniably Spirit-infused ministry.

Not every child will go on to do all that L.R. Scarborough did, but his story is here presented as a case study for what good parenting can produce. Certainly, God's calling is of utmost importance in Scarborough's story, and the power of the Holy Spirit in his life and ministry cannot be disregarded, but even so, George and Martha Scarborough's influence is undeniable, for indeed they did right by their son, and countless lives have been impacted for eternity as a result. George and Martha's spiritual investment has produced a spiritual legacy too great for anyone this side of

---

[8]Ibid., 26.

heaven to measure, and the impact of Martha's cradle-side prayer can still be felt today.

So how can you become the kind of parent that George and Martha Scarborough were? How can you spiritually invest in your children so that they will go on to become faithful followers of God, instruments in His hands for His redemptive purposes? How can you experience the joy that the Scarboroughs had when they received word that Lee had surrendered to the call to preach, in direct answer to their prayers?

The authors of this volume believe that Scripture speaks to every aspect of parenting—and, indeed, to all of life—and so we assert that when the Word of God is properly obeyed, anyone can become this kind of parent. Certainly, God's exact plans differ for every child, but Scripture clearly reveals that He has a specific will by which all parents are to live. We, therefore, have composed the following pages in order to explore just what that will is so that our readers may become thoroughly equipped by the words of God Himself to raise up their children in the training and instruction of the Lord.

Why *Everyday Parenting*?

The authors of this work—faculty, alumni, and friends of Southwestern Baptist Theological Seminary—have no delusions about the number of parenting books that exist in the world today. Many of these are useful resources, with some even appealing to Scripture as the basis for their teaching. So why is this volume necessary?

A Worthy Pursuit

First, learning all that one can about the parenting task is not an unwise pursuit.[9] At least two reasons can be cited. Number one, children are valuable in the eyes of God.

---

[9]For obvious reasons, this book is written mainly for those who have children or plan to have children. But while this would seem to exclude singles and childless couples from the intended audience, consider Paul's instruction in

Psalm 127:3-5a says, "Behold, children are a gift of the Lord, the fruit of the womb is a reward. Like arrows in the hand of a warrior, so are the children of one's youth. How blessed is the man whose quiver is full of them." This passage explicitly identifies children as a gift from the Lord. Renowned preacher Charles Spurgeon, in his commentary on this psalm, writes, "Hence note, 'tis one of the greatest outward blessings to have a family full of dutiful children. To have many children is the next blessing to much grace. To have many children about us is better than to have much wealth about us."[10]

This means that, contrary to what popular culture teaches us about children, they are not accidents, burdens, or inconveniences. Pregnancy, by implication, is not a possibility to be dreaded—as many modern films and television series would have you believe—but rather a blessing to be celebrated.

The very next psalm continues this theme. The psalmist writes, "How blessed is everyone who fears the Lord, who walks in His ways. ... Your wife shall be like a fruitful vine within your house, your children like olive plants around your table. Behold, for thus shall the man be blessed who fears the Lord" (Psalm 128:1, 3-4). Again, we see that children are a blessing. That is, God blesses those who fear Him and walk in His ways, and one manifestation of that blessing is an abundance of children.

Regarding the picture of parents and children gathered around the family table, Spurgeon writes, "Here we have the vine and olive blended—joy from the fruitful wife, and solid comfort from the growing family; these are the choicest products earth can yield: our

---

1 Thessalonians 5:14 and Colossians 4:5-6 for all believers to be ready to offer counsel to those in need. In light of these verses, even singles and childless couples should be prepared for the opportunity, should it arise, to provide counsel from God's Word to those who need it (in this case, parents). Such opportunities could entail pointing a believer in the right direction or even opening a door for evangelism with a nonbeliever.
[10]C.H. Spurgeon, *The Treasury of David*, Vol. 3 (McLean, VA: MacDonald Publishing Company, 1990), 93.

families are gardens of the Lord."[11] While rearing children (especially "an abundance" of them) undoubtedly presents challenges, the clear opinion of God is that we are to cherish such a task.

So, learning about parenting is a worthy pursuit because God values children, and this means parents should as well. And if parents truly value their children as God does, then they should want to be as equipped as possible to parent them.

The second reason learning about parenting is a worthy pursuit is because, in line with God's valuing children, He also places significant weight on the parenting task itself. In Ephesians 6:4, Paul writes by inspiration of the Holy Spirit, "Fathers, do not provoke your children to anger, but bring them up in the discipline and instruction of the Lord." In a parallel passage, he states the same principle this way: "Fathers, do not exasperate your children, so that they will not lose heart" (Colossians 3:21).

These two passages affirm that parents have a responsibility to spiritually nurture their children, raising them up in the discipline—or "training" (NIV)—and instruction—or "admonition" (KJV)—of God. Indeed, if they fail in this task, they risk causing their children to "lose heart," a concept also translated as "become discouraged" (NIV).

As Scarborough said in his quote above, parents can greatly help or hinder God in the matter of their children becoming faithful followers of Him, and these verses affirm such a notion. Whether they help or hinder depends on whether they accept the God-given responsibility of nurturing their children properly.

Deuteronomy 6 provides a more elaborate picture of the spiritual responsibility God places upon parents. In verses 4-9, Moses declares:

> Hear, O Israel! The Lord is our God, the Lord is one! You shall love the Lord your God with all your heart and with all your soul and with all your might. These words, which I am commanding you today, shall be

---

[11]Ibid., 99.

on your heart. You shall teach them diligently to your
sons and shall talk of them when you sit in your house
and when you walk by the way and when you lie down
and when you rise up. You shall bind them as a sign on
your hand and they shall be as frontals on your fore-
head. You shall write them on the doorposts of your
house and on your gates.[12]

Here, Moses shares with the Israelites one of the most foundational truths of their (and our) faith—that God, who has just
redeemed them from slavery in Egypt (as He has redeemed us
from slavery to sin), is the one true God, and they are to love
Him with every ounce of their being.[13] And who is made responsible for teaching such a significant truth to the children among
them? Preachers? Sunday School teachers? Youth pastors? On
the contrary, while these people surely have much to offer, the
responsibility is placed on the shoulders of parents.

Specifically, verse 7 says, "You shall teach [these words] diligently to your sons and shall talk of them when you sit in your
house and when you walk by the way and when you lie down and
when you rise up." Among the Israelites, parents were responsible
for teaching their children the fundamental truths of the faith,
and they were directed to talk about them, essentially, at all times.
These words were continually to be on their lips. We should not
take this to mean that every word coming out of a parent's mouth
was to be sermonic in nature, but whether by implication or expli-
cation, parents were continually to teach their children the truths
of the faith, because they were responsible for doing so. In light

---

[12]Due to the foundational nature of this particular passage, as well as certain
other Scriptures cited in this introduction, multiple chapters in this volume
appeal to these same verses through the lens of their respective subjects.
Hopefully, readers will not find this redundant, for the intention is to allow
readers to achieve greater understanding of God's Word by expounding and
applying the biblical teaching in different contexts.
[13]Jesus later identifies this as the "great and foremost" commandment (Matthew 22:37-38).

of Ephesians 6:4 and Colossians 3:21, this evidently remains the case today for all believers.

Multiple proverbs also speak to parents' importance in the spiritual development of their children. Proverbs 22:6 instructs parents to "train up a child in the way he should go" and assures that "even when he is old he will not depart from it." Proverbs 22:15 and 23:13-14 address the issue of discipline, noting that by it parents can "remove" foolishness from the hearts of their children and even "rescue" their souls "from Sheol." Clearly, parents wield significant influence and, by extension, responsibility in regard to the spiritual upbringing of their children.

Though more Scriptures could be cited, these select few are sufficient to conclude that God attributes great importance to the duty of parents to teach their children to obey His Word.[14] If God places so much weight on this responsibility, why would we not want to consume as many biblically rooted resources as possible in order to become as equipped as we can possibly be?

A Text-Driven Resource

The second defense for this volume is the authors' desire to produce a parenting resource that is driven by the text of Scripture. We believe the Bible is the authoritative, sufficient, inspired, and inerrant Word of the Creator of the universe Himself. We also believe, as has already been stated, that God, the very Author of life, has spoken through this Word to every aspect of parenting imaginable—if not directly, then indirectly. We have therefore set out to explore and pass on what God has said in the Scriptures about the parenting task so that our readers—assuming they put

---

[14]This does not mean, of course, that we should brainwash our children to the extent that they become robots, mindlessly regurgitating the Christian doctrines we have impressed on them. On the contrary, it means we expose them to that which is true—the Word of God—and show them through both words and actions how the Creator of all things would have us live out the full and abundant lives we have in Christ.

this teaching into practice[15]—may raise their children in a biblically informed manner.

Here are a few Scriptures that attest to the Bible's reliability, sufficiency, and superiority to anything else the world has to offer:

> All Scripture is inspired by God and profitable for teaching, for reproof, for correction, for training in righteousness; so that the man of God may be adequate, equipped for *every good work*. (2 Timothy 3:16-17, emphasis added)

> ... seeing that His divine power has granted to us *everything pertaining to life and godliness*, through the true knowledge of Him who called us by His own glory and excellence. For by these He has granted to us His precious and magnificent promises, so that by them you may become partakers of the divine nature, having escaped the corruption that is in the world by lust. (2 Peter 1:3-4, emphasis added)

> For the word of God is living and active and sharper than any two-edged sword, and piercing as far as the division of soul and spirit, of both joints and marrow, and able to judge the thoughts and intentions of the heart. (Hebrews 4:12)

As with the previous section, this list of relevant Scriptures could go on and on, but suffice it to say in summary that the Bible

---

[15]Consider Jesus' words from Matthew 7:24-27: "Therefore everyone who hears these words of Mine *and acts on them*, may be compared to a wise man who built his house on the rock. And the rain fell, and the floods came, and the winds blew and slammed against that house; and yet it did not fall, for it had been founded on the rock. Everyone who hears these words of Mine *and does not act on them*, will be like a foolish man who built his house on the sand. The rain fell, and the floods came, and the winds blew and slammed against that house; and it fell—and great was its fall" (emphasis added).

is the very Word of God and provides us with everything we need to partake of the divine nature. Furthermore, nothing known to man is able to see, discern, and expose man to the degree that Scripture is.

With this as our foundation, we have composed this volume as a text-driven resource, our aim being to illuminate what God has revealed in His Word about the numerous aspects of the parenting task. Therefore, everything contained herein is ultimately tied back to Scripture and, by extension, to God Himself.

Issues in Parenting

The final defense for this volume is its approach. The work covers a wide range of issues in parenting, and each of the chapters is written by someone with experience and/or direct training in the particular matter about which he has written. This means that, while all the teaching contained herein is rooted in Scripture, it is also informed by experience and is thus offered by those with unique insight into the relevant issues.

Here is an overview of the work:

- In chapter 1, Evan and Melanie Lenow lay the groundwork for a text-driven philosophy of parenting. Using Proverbs 4 as their primary reference, the Lenows examine the wisdom Solomon passed on to his son in order to determine how parents today can raise their children to walk in righteousness. In so doing, the Lenows also uncover the truth that parenting is a sanctifying process whereby parents grow in selflessness, humility, and knowledge of God. *Lenow serves as associate professor of ethics at Southwestern Seminary. He and Melanie have four children.*

- Chapter 2 addresses the topic of evangelism in the home. Kelly A. King provides practical help for parents to lay an intentional foundation for their children's belief in God's Word as well as specific ways they can help their children begin and grow in their personal relationships with Christ. *King earned both her Master of Arts in Religious Education and Ph.D. from Southwestern Seminary (in 1992 and 2009, respectively). She serves as children's minister at Magnolia Church in Riverside, California.*

- Building on the foundation of chapter 2, chapter 3 tackles the subject of spiritual formation through family worship. How can parents practically go about establishing a time of worship in their home with their immediate family, and why is such a practice necessary to begin with? Drawing from Scripture as well as their own personal experience, Malcolm and Karen Yarnell answer these questions. *Yarnell serves as research professor of systematic theology at Southwestern. He and Karen have five children.*

- Chapter 4 deals with the subject of raising men in a culture of boys. Dean Nichols appeals to the book of Proverbs for wisdom in this matter and explores Solomon's instructions for raising sons to be "wise" men rather than "fools." Nichols also addresses discipline, alcohol, and the frightening prospect of a child becoming a "prodigal son." *Nichols serves as Southwestern Seminary's chaplain. He and his wife Mary have nine children.*

- As a complement to chapter 4, chapter 5 addresses the subject of raising girls in a sex-saturated culture. Mark and Carmen Howell offer a brief examination of today's culture—which they point out is no friend to our children—and then explore the solution: raising girls in such a way that God becomes their greatest desire. *Howell serves as senior pastor of Hunters Glen Baptist Church in Plano, Texas. He and Carmen have two daughters.*

- In chapter 6, Justin and Sarah Buchanan explore how parents can raise their children—particularly once they reach their teenage years—to live on mission for God, joining with Christ to seek and save the lost. *Buchanan serves as assistant professor of student ministry at Southwestern. He and Sarah have five children.*

- Chapter 7 deals with the question of education. Namely, should children be educated via public school, private school, or home school? Charles and Monica Patrick briefly explore the history of education in America, examine what God's Word says about education, and then provide a rubric by which parents can choose a mode of education for their children. *Patrick serves as vice president for strategic initiatives and communications at Southwestern Seminary as well as executive editor of Seminary Hill Press. He and Monica have four children.*

- Chapter 8 examines the subject of raising children with special needs. David-Lafe and Katie Frugé relate their own experience of raising two daughters with special needs and reveal why special-needs families need the church and why the church needs special-needs families. The Frugés also broach the topic of being pro-life in a pro-abortion world. *The Frugés are Ph.D. students at Southwestern Seminary. They have two daughters.*

- In chapter 9, Mark Leeds shares his testimony of adopting three children and relates the biblical principles that aided him and his wife in raising their kids beyond the adoption day. *Leeds serves as registrar and assistant professor of systematic theology at Southwestern. He and his wife Jennifer have three children.*

- Chapter 10 provides wisdom on what to do when your child struggles with homosexuality. Johnny Derouen's more than 40 years of experience in student and now pastoral ministry have seen him walk with parents through this heart-wrenching issue, and here he shares biblical teaching on the severity of sin and the need of every believer for forgiveness through Christ. *Derouen is pastor of the First Baptist Church of Muskogee, Oklahoma. He earned his Master of Arts in Religious Education (1993) and Ph.D. (2005) from Southwestern Seminary, where he served for a time as associate professor of student ministry.*

- In chapter 11, Robin Covington relates lessons she learned from raising her children in a cross-cultural context. As missionaries to Russia, Robin and her husband Randy discovered that while rearing children in a different culture presents challenges, ultimately, placing children in the Lord's hands remains of utmost importance. *Robin earned her diploma in Christian education from Southwestern in 1999, and Randy completed his Master of Arts in Religious Education and Ph.D. at Southwestern in 1984 and 2004, respectively. They served as missionaries for the International Mission Board for 22 years—14 in Russia and eight in the Balkans. They now live in Alaska, where Randy serves as executive director of the Alaska Baptist Convention. They have two children.*

- Chapter 12 addresses the difficult subject of losing a child. Matt Miller reflects on his own experience of enduring such a trial and relates the biblical comforts that helped him and his wife persevere through it. *Miller serves as director of communications and marketing at Southwestern Seminary. His wife Natalie completed her Master of Arts in Missiology at the seminary in 2003. They have two children.*

Some of these chapters are more experience-based, whereas others are more research-based. Likewise, some are more expositional while others are more application-focused. Regardless, all are written to be accessible to scholars and laypersons alike.

The authors acknowledge the existence of other works that cover some of these same topics, but these are presented here so that (a) readers will have concise and easily digestible coverage of the given topics, and (b) readers will have access to biblical teaching on all of these subjects through a single, easily navigable volume. Our hope is that these efforts make the process of becoming biblically informed and educated on these various aspects of the parenting task as smooth and convenient as possible.

Hoisting the Next Generation upon Our Shoulders

Not long after surrendering to God's call to preach, L.R. Scarborough delivered his first sermon in the First Baptist Church of Abilene, Texas. His father George was understandably eager to hear his youngest son's first message, and so he sat three or four rows from the pulpit so that he could have a good view.

When Lee's sermon was underway and he had begun to display the fiery passion for which he would later become well known, a woman sitting directly in front of George leaned over to the woman next to her and said, "He's surpassing his father, isn't he?"

This remark surely inspired a smile to spread across George's face. He was not jealous at the remark; on the contrary, he was likely filled with exuberant pride. Indeed, his years of spiritually investing in his child, raising him up in "the way he should go," were beginning to yield significant returns before his very eyes. He leaned forward to the women, who apparently did not realize he was there, and said to them, "He ought to beat me, he is standing on my shoulders."

May we all be able to say this of our children. May we hoist them upon our shoulders so that they may accomplish more for the Kingdom of God than we even thought possible. May we move forward in the task of everyday parenting armed with the Sword of the Spirit—the Word of God—so that we may raise up the next generation to be faithful, obedient, and devoted followers of the Lord Jesus Christ. May we, like George and Martha Scarborough, look on with indescribable joy as our children—those for whom we earnestly prayed, even to the detriment of our own bodies—usher countless souls into the Kingdom of God. And may our children eventually do the same for theirs—on and on, from generation to generation, until our blessed Lord returns.

CHAPTER 1

A TEXT-DRIVEN PHILOSOPHY OF PARENTING

By Evan and Melanie Lenow

The word "parenting" brings to mind many words that could be paired alongside it. Wonderful. Exciting. Exhausting. Loving. Frustrating. Joyous. Sweet. Stinky. Gracious. Sacrificial. Heartbreaking. Precious. Blessing. But the one word that has proven to be the overarching theme throughout our parenting adventure is "humbling."

We do not necessarily mean individual incidents that humble a prideful soul—although plenty of those exist. For example, when your young child throws a gallon of milk out of the shopping cart, and it explodes all over the frozen food section with the force of an atomic bomb. Or when your teenage daughter chooses the middle of a clothing store as the best place to loudly discuss the appropriate length of a woman's skirt. These are humbling situations where you hope the floor will open up and swallow both you and your child and transport you quickly back to the privacy of your own home.

Those situations are real, but they are not the extent of parenting as a whole. The humbling experience to which we refer is the constant act of dying to yourself and your personal comforts for the sake and well-being of your children. Thus, parenting is one of the most humbling experiences a person can have.

In every stage of rearing a child, the Lord must work on the heart, mind, and soul of both parents to continue to place them in the position where they can effectively guide their child. We have been on this journey for more than twelve years now, and while there is still much opportunity for successes and mistakes, we have noticed one common thread. The daily act of caring for someone else causes great friction in a heart that primarily wants to tend to its own needs. The friction causes a hard, self-sufficient heart to soften and become moldable, allowing God to work greatly in the life of that parent. With God's tender leading, the parents die to their own selfish tendencies, see their child's needs, and reach out to connect to their child in whatever way is necessary.

In light of dying to our own desires and recognizing the needs of our children, we periodically sit down to consider our goals for the four children whom God has entrusted to us. We have a number of goals along the lines of education, physical activity, and spiritual development. Those goals change over time as our children grow older, but the main focus of those goals remains to see our children grow into responsible, productive members of society who know the truth of the Gospel and follow after Christ with all their hearts.

The one constant in our parenting strategy is that we would be guided by the principles and promises of Scripture. You could call this "text-driven parenting" in the sense that we want our parenting to be the product of our study of Scripture. We lay no claim to being experts in parenting, since our journey as parents is still in-process. However, we want to offer some basic biblical principles that can serve as a philosophy of parenting. In so doing, we want to look at the effects of parenting on both children and parents. Seeing the effects on children may seem obvious, but the effects of parenting on the parents less so. Yet, our conviction is that parents are both humbled and changed in the process of parenting according to God's Word.

Teaching Our Children to Walk in Righteousness

There are a number of passages to which we could turn in order to discuss a biblical philosophy of parenting. Deuteronomy 6:4–9 and Ephesians 6:1–4 immediately come to mind as important passages for discussion. But we want to consider a section of Scripture that is sometimes overlooked in discussions about parenting. For our purposes, we will spend our time in Proverbs 4. Now certainly, the book of Proverbs offers a tremendous amount of wisdom for both parents and children, but we sometimes forget that the book opens with a focus on parenting. It also gives us a beautiful perspective on the ultimate aim in parenting, not simply how to survive the day-to-day grind of shepherding our children.

At least eleven times in the opening eight chapters of Proverbs, Solomon stops to remind his son to listen to his instructions.[16] While space does not permit us to explore all eight of these chapters, we do see that Solomon desperately wants to pass along his wisdom to his son. Considering that Solomon received a wise and discerning heart from the Lord (1 Kings 3:3–14), he clearly had a special gift to pass along to his own child from his wisdom. As such, we are wise to heed Solomon's words ourselves and to pass them along to our own children.

What is Solomon's ultimate aim in passing along his wisdom and instruction to his son? The aim is righteousness. Solomon paints a contrasting picture in these opening chapters of Proverbs, and specifically within chapter 4, that demonstrates the difference between a life of evil and a life of righteousness. The end result of following his instructions is that Solomon's son would walk in "the path of the righteous." This path "is like the light of dawn, that shines brighter and brighter until the full day" (Proverbs 4:18). In the same way, we should desire for our children to become righteous men and women, and it is our responsibility to guide them along that path until they are able to walk it on their own.

---

[16]Proverbs 1:8; 2:1–2; 3:1–2; 4:1–2, 10, 20; 5:1–2; 6:20–21; 7:1–3, 24; 8:32–34.

Being Righteous

What does it mean for our children to be righteous? Righteousness is a matter of being and doing. Being righteous implies the concept of right standing before God and mankind. This comes to us as one of God's attributes that we can exhibit—however imperfectly—because we are made in His image (Genesis 1:26–27). Righteousness thus implies moral perfection, holiness, and justice. Due to the fact that we are fallen and have sinful natures, we cannot be completely righteous in this life. Sin has corrupted us and made us incapable of true righteousness. However, Scripture teaches us that Christ's righteousness has been imputed to us so that we stand before God justified by faith and receive the righteousness of Christ (Romans 5:18–21).

For our children and for us as parents, being righteous means that we have been saved by grace through faith in Jesus Christ. Of course, this raises a very difficult tension for us, because we cannot exercise faith on behalf of our children. We want our children to come to faith in due time, but we also have a responsibility to lead them down a path that resembles a life of faith. Our children spend lots of time in our home, church, and school hearing about God and learning Scripture. This has occasionally made us ponder how they will respond when truly confronted with the Gospel message applied to their own lives. We have often wondered if they would be able to separate the church experience from personal faith in order to see that they need a personal relationship with God.

With our oldest daughter, we were able to see this play out in our own home. One evening, we were talking through Romans 10:9-10 in relation to praying for some missionaries. We asked her how the Bible says people in other countries come to faith in Christ. She responded by quoting Romans 10:9. We applied that same question to lost people in our own country, and she dutifully responded with the same answer. Finally, we applied it to our own family, and she sheepishly gave the same answer. Later that evening, she started asking us questions about her own salvation, recognizing that she had not confessed with her mouth that Jesus is Lord and believed in her heart that God raised Him from the dead. We were then able to lead her to Christ. At that moment, she became righteous.

This is where wisdom and righteousness come together. Solomon's instructions to his son are the embodiment of righteousness. Heeding his instructions ultimately ends in being righteous. In Proverbs 4:7–9, Solomon writes, "Acquire wisdom; and with all your acquiring, get understanding. Prize her, and she will exalt you; she will honor you if you embrace her. She will place on your head a garland of grace; she will present you with a crown of beauty." Notice what Solomon tells his son. When he acquires wisdom and gains understanding, he will be exalted. Wisdom will honor him and place upon his head a garland of grace and a crown of beauty. Here, Solomon is speaking of more than just actions. He speaks of virtue. Our wise instructions to our children should ultimately lead to a life characterized by righteousness.

We must recognize that our ultimate goal is not simply the salvation of our children, because we cannot bring that to fruition—only the Holy Spirit can do that. Instead, our goal should be to instill in our children a life of righteousness. True righteousness is found only in Christ, but wise parenting will lead our children to the truth of the Gospel so that they may hear and believe. In so doing, we will be those with beautiful feet "who bring good news of good things" (Romans 10:14–15).

Doing Righteousness

The other side of the righteousness equation is "doing." Much of Solomon's instruction to his son in Proverbs 4 focuses on the aspect of doing righteousness. He begins this focus in verse 4, which reads, "Let your heart hold fast my words; keep my commandments and live." The emphasis is on following instructions. Later in the chapter, Solomon offers negative commands, which is how we often articulate ideas to our children. He says, "Do not enter the path of the wicked and do not proceed in the way of evil men. Avoid it, do not pass by it; turn away from it and pass on" (4:14–15). He goes on to offer some specific examples about deceitful words (4:24), sexual immorality (5:3–23), debt (6:1), and slothfulness (6:6–11). These negative instructions assist in setting boundaries for Solomon's son in his actions.

One of the first steps in helping our children do righteousness is to avoid doing unrighteousness. We often follow this pattern when parenting younger children. For example, we give instructions to our younger children with the expectation that they will follow them. These instructions may involve such things as not running into the street or not touching the hot stove. The instructions are short and simple and often articulated negatively—"don't do this or that." Our children do not always understand the reasoning behind those instructions, but the commands are for their safety. These negative commands help younger children know their limits and understand what may harm them.

Solomon does not end with negative prohibitions against unrighteousness. He also affirms that his son should walk in righteousness through particular actions. He writes, "Watch over your heart with all diligence, for from it flow the springs of life. ... Let your eyes look directly ahead and let your gaze be fixed straight in front of you. Watch the path of your feet and all your ways will be established" (Proverbs 4:23, 25–26). While negative prohibitions may dominate our parenting of younger children, we change to more positive instructions with our older children. Unlike telling our younger children to avoid touching the stove altogether, we tell our older children to turn on the stove and start cooking. They are able to go out into the street for an intended purpose as long as they are aware of their surroundings and avoid the dangers of moving vehicles.

We also transition to giving reasons for our instructions. We may explain why our children should take certain actions and avoid others. Solomon follows this same pattern in Proverbs 4. For example, he tells his son,

> My son, give attention to my words; incline your ear
> to my sayings. Do not let them depart from your sight;
> keep them in the midst of your heart. For they are life
> to those who find them and health to all their body.
> Watch over your heart with all diligence, for from it
> flow the springs of life. (4:20–23)

His instructions to do righteousness lead to a life that is righteous. His wise parental instruction is life and health. They create a righteous heart from which springs forth life.

The ultimate goal of parenting is for our children to walk in righteousness. We are to lead our children to both be righteous and do righteousness. You cannot have one without the other—to perform righteous actions without living a righteous life is pharisaic; a righteous life without righteous actions is hypocritical.

One of the best ways to teach this righteousness to our children is to model it for them. This is where the effect of parenting on the parents becomes reality. In our efforts to teach our children to walk in righteousness, we must walk in righteousness ourselves.

Training Ourselves to Walk in Righteousness

Coming home with a newborn child is a life-altering experience, but the most vivid experience was leaving the hospital with our firstborn. We were excited to get home and start our new life as a little family. However, our main thought was, "The nurses are really going to let us leave with her. They don't know us or our qualifications. No one from the hospital is going to stop by and check on us. They have full confidence in us that we are going to keep her alive and well."

We were astonished. At that point, all we had done was read a few books and babysit a few times. In our minds, it was the equivalent of entrusting a young pilot to fly an airplane with only a Chuck E. Cheese arcade game to prepare him. Yes, we each had a master's degree by that time, but we were ignorant about what it meant to take care of this little one. Years passed and, with only minor blunders, we kept her alive and cared for and loved. But then that sweet baby became a toddler and then a kindergartener and now a pre-teen. At every stage, we have felt like we did as we first left the hospital—completely unsure of the future and uncertain of our ability to raise her. This illustrates the fact that parenting is a growing process for the parents as well as the children.

Parenting grows and molds the parent. It is obvious that how we parent affects our children, but we would argue that the effects of parenting on the mother and father are just as great, if not even greater.

We each begin on the same playing field. We are sinners in need of a Savior. Once we accept Christ as Lord of our lives and trust Him as our Savior, we still have a long way to go in our own sanctification. When God calls believers to be parents, He is beckoning them to join Him on a long, slow walk to maturity and righteousness. As we parent our children, the Lord uses the events of each day to grow, teach, and mature us. The threads of the fabric of our lives are greatly made up from the experiences of rearing children.

At the end of the day, parenting trains us to walk in righteousness as we model that righteousness to our children. Three areas in which parenting changed us are selflessness, lifelong covenant, and godly wisdom.

Selflessness

When we think about maturity in parenting, our focus tends to be on seeing our children grow into mature adults. However, as parents, we benefit from the maturity that comes in shepherding the children God has given us. In Proverbs 4:3-4, Solomon reminds us that he, too, had to grow up into the wise parent he had become. He writes, "When I was a son to my father, tender and the only son in the sight of my mother, then he taught me and said to me, 'Let your heart hold fast to my words; keep my commandments and live.'" Solomon did not become a wise and mature parent overnight. He benefited from the instruction of his own parents and the wisdom that God had given him. In an act of selflessness, he then passed that wisdom to his own son. We need the benefits of wisdom in our own lives to push us past the point of considering only our own desires to focusing on the needs of others.[17]

Incorporating other people's needs into our daily lives and decision-making causes us to act less impulsively. God uses our children to take the focus off of ourselves and put it on others.

In our culture, a general sign of maturity is getting married and starting a family. Why is this? It is because our decisions take on more gravity when we are considering the well-being of another person. Upon getting married, we no longer asked, "What is the best decision for me?" Rather, we asked, "What is the best decision for us?" After we had our first child, the focus then shifted to include more people. This forced us into maturity and a state of selflessness.

Just because a person does not have a family of his own, does not mean he is irresponsible or selfish. Instead, there is a freedom that a single person has that a married person, especially with children, does not have. Paul even speaks of the benefit of being single, because then, one is able to focus on doing the Lord's work without the concerns of a family (1 Corinthians 7:7–8, 25–35). However, in the same vein, the Lord uses the commitment of a family to mature the parents by having them settle down and develop roots for their family. The commitment of the home becomes more important than anything that takes place outside the home.

Personally, this was a difficult area of maturity for me (Melanie). Growing up and even in early adulthood, I was always the first to volunteer for an adventure. I constantly looked for the next new ministry to join. I was the first to volunteer and the first to sign up for a mission trip. The Lord used these passions and experiences

---

[17]See Philippians 2:3-4—"Do nothing from selfishness or empty conceit, but with humility of mind regard one another as more important than yourselves; do not merely look out for your own personal interests, but also for the interests of others."

greatly in my life. However, after I was married and especially after we began to have children, God began to teach me the beauty of staying. Instead of always being the one to go, God called me to be the one to support and send others. Some think the challenge is in the going, but for me, it is harder to stay. I still have some of the opportunities I had before, but it is much more complicated to leave town or move locations than it was for me twenty years ago.

The Lord has used the commitment of our family to grow within us steadfastness, patience, joy for others, and commitment. Those lessons in maturity were made possible because our actions now affect four other people, so we can no longer just do what we think is best for us as a couple or as individuals, but only what is best for all of us. Dying to our own desires and humbling ourselves to serve our family has been monumental in becoming who we are today.

Lifelong Covenant

A second way that we believe the Lord uses parenting to shape us is through the realization that parenting is the only long-term job that no one else can do. God gave each child one mother and one father. Through simple biology, we can see this is the way God ordained it.

Of course, sin has horribly tarnished the concept of family. Whether it is through death, divorce, poor choices on the part of the parents, or some other tragedy, not all children have the privilege of being raised by both parents. However, that does not change the fact that this is the way God originally intended it to be.

Parenting is the only job that no one else can do for us. Are you a brilliant student? Someone will eventually come along who has studied more. Are you successful in your job? Someone, somewhere is just as successful at hers. Are you the best volunteer at your church? God will raise up someone to step into your role when you step down.

These accomplishments are not bad things, but our point is that every other accomplishment we achieve, every other job we have, and every other hat we wear can be filled by someone else.

However, no one can be your child's mother but you, Mom. No one can be your child's father but you, Dad. On the good days and the bad days, you are it. You might want to throw in the towel, but you cannot. No one is waiting in the wings to take over. We believe this is an important concept that God uses to grow us as parents.

Let us look again at Solomon's words to his son. Each time he introduces his instructions, the focus is on a personal relationship. The first time he calls for his son's attention, he states, "Hear, my son, your father's instruction and do not forsake your mother's teaching" (Proverbs 1:8). From that point forward, the constant refrain is "my son." In chapter 4, he even reflects on his own relationship with his father and mother and their teachings (4:3).

This phrase reminds me (Evan) of what has become an endearing way to refer to our only son. Of all the nicknames he has been given by us and his sisters, my favorite is what I call him most often—"Son." That simple word reminds me of how my father often called me by that same name (and still does to this day). It is a name that implies a unique relationship. It is a relationship founded in biology but that extends far beyond what either parent or child can comprehend.

We do not know at what point in his life Solomon penned these words to his son, but they have a lasting impact that transcends any concept of age. The relationship of parent and child is lifelong.

The moment God blessed us with each of our children, we entered a lifelong covenant with them that we cannot undo. One of the many benefits of this commitment is the mandate to make it work. How do we make it work? Certainly, not in our own strength.

Basically, every parent is in a lifelong commitment that cannot be dissolved. It is hard and challenging and will bring extreme joy as well as extreme frustration. In our own power, we do not have the strength to succeed or even endure. The only way to go about parenting is through the power of God.

In His magnificent wisdom, God places us as parents in a relationship with our children where the only pathway to success is our total reliance on Him. If it were easy, we would do it alone. But God wants us to depend on Him because it strengthens our relationship with Him. God uses our lifelong parenting commitment to our children to increase our lifelong dependence on Him.

It takes a humble heart to admit that we need someone else to help. But at the moment we come to that realization, God steps in and not only helps but empowers us to be so much more for our children.

Godly Wisdom

The final way that parenting changes us is that, through it, God leads us into a deeper knowledge of Him. Solomon writes, "The fear of the Lord is the beginning of wisdom, and the knowledge of the Holy One is understanding" (Proverbs 9:10). To become wise parents, we must become God-fearing people. Fear of God in this situation means a heightened awareness, reverence, or being in awe. As much as we love books and education and treasure a godly friend's advice, our wisdom will never increase with those tools as much as it will increase with growing in the fear of the Lord. Fearing the Lord means trusting His Word. Fearing the Lord means acting on His commands. Fearing the Lord means striving to know Him more.

Solomon clearly wanted to communicate to his son what he believed would make him successful in life. Solomon had so much to offer as the ruler of a great kingdom, a successful businessman, and a shrewd politician. However, the instructions he conveyed to his son came from godly wisdom. He wanted his son to walk in righteousness by following God.

This was not something that Solomon had conjured up on his own; it came from the wisdom God had given him so he would not trust in his own strength. Solomon illustrates this is Proverbs 3:5–7 when he writes, "Trust in the Lord with all your heart and do not lean on your own understanding. In all your ways acknowledge Him, and He will make your paths straight. Do not be wise in your own eyes; fear the Lord and turn away from evil."

In the end, Solomon was relying on the wisdom of God to advise his own son for the future. In the same way, we must rely on God's wisdom for our own children. In doing so, we will be changed ourselves to trust more upon God.

When our oldest daughter was a baby, there were moments when I (Melanie) was overwrought with anxiety. I functioned fine on a daily basis, but out of nowhere, irrational fears would overcome me. Most of the time, I feared overlooking something or making a mistake that would hurt our daughter.

One day, the Lord gave me the verse, "For God has not given us a spirit of timidity, but of power and love and discipline" (2 Timothy 1:7). If I was going to grow as a mother, if I was going to grow in my wisdom as a parent, I had to grow in my fear of the Lord. I had to trust that He gave me a sound mind. I had to trust that God loved me and enabled me to love my daughter. I had to believe the fear I was feeling was not given to me by the Lord. I had to know Him more than I knew all the things that could go wrong with my child. I was able to overcome that spiritual battle and mature as a mother by fearing the Lord more and trusting in His wisdom.

The best source of godly wisdom is God's Word. We can seek counsel from many different sources, but the only infallible source of truth in parenting and all of life is Scripture. When we face the fears and frustrations of parenting, we can rely on God's faithful Word to give us the wisdom we need to rear the precious children He has given us.

With Wisdom Comes Humility

As mentioned previously, we do not have all the answers. Our journey as parents is still in the middle stages. We still have much to learn. That is part of what makes writing a chapter like this so difficult. Even after a lifetime of parenting, we believe that there will be some answers that still escape our comprehension. Yet, at the same time, we trust that our Heavenly Father exemplifies the model of what it means to parent our children. He is our Father, and through His example communicated in His Word and lived out in our lives, we see how to be parents.

It is often fun for us to watch new parents now that we have been on this parenting journey for a while. We all start the journey from basically the same place of not knowing what it is going to look like. As the years go by, we hopefully mature and grow in our understanding of parenting. Along the way, we figure out that we know much less than we ever thought.

As believers, we trust that God will give us grace to parent in such a way that our children see and hear the message of the Gospel. In the end, we are humbled because we know that we could never do it without God's help.

The high calling of being a parent pushes us to humble ourselves and seek God as our ultimate guide and leader. As we grow in our knowledge of Him, He will give us the wisdom we need to rear our children for His glory.

CHAPTER 2

EVANGELISM IN YOUR HOME

By Kelly A. King

Think about your children's physical nourishment. Certainly, you did not wait until your children could feed themselves before giving them food. You did not wait until they could understand the food pyramid before introducing them to healthy eating habits. As your children grew, you took care to make sure they were getting the right kinds of nutrients from a variety of sources. You made decisions for them in order to help them be as healthy as possible.

So it is with your children's spiritual growth. You need not wait until your children can read the Bible for themselves before introducing them to God's Word, God's promises, and God's great gift of Jesus to the world.

Since the days of Moses, God has commanded the retelling of the stories of His might, grace, and love to children.[18] Both the Old and New Testaments are filled with commands and instructions on obeying God's commands and teaching them to others, and this includes children. In Scripture, children are observed as "having the ability to comprehend something of the things of God."[19] Concerning the Shema and other exhortations to parents

---

[18]Portions of this chapter are adapted from chapter 1 of Kelly A. King, "A Comparative Analysis of Children's Cognitive and Affective Learning from Selected Bible Story Videos" (Ph.D. diss., Southwestern Baptist Theological Seminary, 2009).

[19]Roy B. Zuck, *Precious in His Sight: Childhood and Children in the Bible* (Grand Rapids, MI: Baker Books, 1996), 19.

throughout Deuteronomy, Zuck asks, "If children were not able to understand and respond to divine truths, why would God have given these commands to parents?"[20]

As a parent, part of your job is to "repeat"[21] God's commands to your children and help them understand who God is and what He has done for us—most specifically through sending Jesus as our Savior.

Be Intentional and Make a Plan

Parents who want to evangelize their children should begin with a clear understanding of the term. Matt Queen, who occupies the L.R. Scarborough Chair of Evangelism at Southwestern Baptist Theological Seminary, defines evangelism as "that Spirit-empowered activity in which the disciples of Jesus Christ give a complete and intentional witness to the life, death, burial, and resurrection of Jesus Christ, calling unbelievers to become disciples of Jesus Christ by repenting of their sins and placing their faith in Jesus Christ alone."[22]

There are no "junior rules" for becoming a Christian. Romans 10:9—"that if you confess with your mouth Jesus as Lord, and believe in your heart that God raised Him from the dead, you will be saved"—does not come with a separate clause for children.

Nevertheless, as you make your plans to share intentionally the good news of Christ with the children in your care, keep 1 Corinthians 13:11 in view: "When I was a child, I used to speak like a child, think like a child, reason like a child; when I became a man, I did away with childish things." As you lay a foundation for your children's understanding and practices related to, prayerfully one

---

[20]Ibid.

[21]*The Believer's Study Bible, New King James Version*, Ed., W.A. Criswell (Nashville, TN: Thomas Nelson Publishers, 1991), Study notes, 256.

[22]Matt Queen, *Everyday Evangelism* (Fort Worth, TX: Seminary Hill Press, 2015), 15.

day, their personal relationship with Christ, keep in mind what vocabulary and cognitive skills will be developmentally sustainable.

You may quickly tell a coworker you are scheduled for an appendectomy next week, but conveying the same thoughts to a young child will take a different vocabulary and decidedly more time. You will still be having the same operation, but instead of a quick remark, you will need to explain that you are going to the hospital so that some doctors can operate on you to take out a part of your body (appendix) that is sick. The doctor is probably going to give you some stiches and bandages to help you heal, and you might not be able to play hide and seek for a few days, etc.

So, in this example, the procedure and outcome are the same, but the vocabulary is translated for a child. Referring to Proverbs 22:6,[23] Franz Delitzch notes that instructional methods should be adjusted "according to the stage of life, and its peculiarities; the method ought to be arranged according to the degree of development which the mental and bodily life of the [child] has arrived at."[24]

Study after study reveals that parents are the most important faith influences for growing children and adolescents. Use this information to your advantage and be intentional about what you are teaching your children. The remainder of this chapter provides specific ways you can intentionally lay a strong foundation for your children's belief in God's Word and its promises as well as ways you can help your children begin and grow in their personal relationships with Christ.

Consider each spiritual discipline you are building up for your children to be the groundwork for their understanding of and trust in Christ. Specifically, you will want to be cognizant of times when you can help your children understand the concept of sin, who Jesus is, and how when Jesus died on the cross, He was taking

---

[23]"Train up a child in the way he should go, even when he is old he will not depart from it."
[24]Franz Delitzch, *Biblical Commentary on the Proverbs of Solomon* (Charleston, SC: BiblioBazaar, 2009), 86-87.

the punishment for your children's (and everyone's) sins so that a relationship with Jesus now as well as in eternity is available to all who confess Christ as Savior and Lord.

Each child is unique and has affinities and interests that are different from other boys and girls in his same age group. If you have more than one child, you have already noticed that even though they are being reared in the same household, they have different likes and dislikes, different ways of expressing themselves, different ways of communicating, and different ways of receiving praise and instruction. Before you move on to the next few pages, take a moment to make a short list for each child in your care related to what really piques his interest, what struggles he is facing, and what truths from God's Word might be most meaningful to him at this time.[25]

For each of the following instructions, commands, or directives from God's Word, think about how these might manifest themselves in your home with intentionality.

Set an Example of Purity and Kindness for Your Children

Finally, brethren, whatever is true, whatever is honorable, whatever is right, whatever is pure, whatever is lovely, whatever is of good repute, if there is any excellence and if anything worthy of praise, dwell on these things.
(Philippians 4:8)

Paul's exhortation to the Philippians to "dwell on these things" goes beyond "simple thought. The church was to count on these things and to chart its course according to them."[26] Fee suggests that one should look for what is true, uplifting, and admirable in all that culture has to offer "with a discriminating eye."[27]

---

[25]See Appendix A for a sample chart.
[26]Richard R. Melick, Jr., *The New American Commentary: Philippians, Colossians, and Philemon* (Nashville, TN: Broadman Press, 1991), 150.
[27]Gordon D. Fee, *Paul's Letters to the Philippians, New International Commentary on the New Testament* (Grand Rapids, MI: William B. Eerdmans Publishing Co., 1995), 421.

To ask children to speak or act in ways that are inconsistent with what they see their parents doing will be difficult. So, the first step to evangelizing children in your own home is to be certain of your own relationship with Christ. Is it strong? Are you actively working to strengthen it? Are you practicing the spiritual disciplines you hope to instill in your children?

Thankfully, you do not have to be perfect to "train up a child in the way he should go," but you do need to make sure to the best of your ability you are not behaving or endorsing activities that are in direct opposition to Scripture. This includes how you choose to spend your free time, what you read, and what you watch on television and social media. Then be cognizant of times when you can lay a foundation for understanding and when you can explicitly make a connection to God's desire for your children to have a personal relationship with Him.

When parents want to help their children learn how to play an instrument or play a sport, they usually start with the basics—how to throw a ball, how to read music, how to suit up for the task at hand. Some parents may find it helpful to think about spiritual growth in the same way. Trying to explain all the attributes of God to a toddler is going to be challenging and ineffective if you talk to him as if he were in seminary. Start with the basics and help your child understand what unconditional love is even before he knows what those words mean. Tell your children as often as needed, "I love you ... no matter what."

Before your children can read, make connections between their everyday lives and God's love for them. Something as simple as walking in the yard and saying, "God made the flowers. Thank you, God, for everything you made." Pointing to the moon and stars, you can say, "God made the stars. Thank you, God, for the beautiful stars." When you look at the picture gallery of family members in your home, you can say, "God gave us families. Thank you, God, for Grandma!" When you notice your child being kind to a friend at church or school, you can say, "The Bible tells us to love one another. That was nice how you helped Olivia pick up her papers."

You can continue to make connections between everyday life and God's plans for our lives after your children learn to read in the same way, as well as by expanding on that to include specific Scripture references or having conversations about what your child has discovered from God's Word.

For example, if your child is facing a challenge with friends at school or on her soccer team, you can say, "Jesus told His disciples to be 'shrewd as serpents and innocent as doves' (Matthew 10:16). Let's think of some ways you can respond to your friends that satisfy these instructions." Helping children discover responses combining "shrewdness and integrity"[28] throughout their lives will nurture both their relationship with God and their relationship with you.

Applications in this regard are virtually endless—just be sure you are using Scripture as a way to encourage reliance on God's Word and not solely for winning an argument or justifying your own actions all the time. The point is to encourage boys and girls to turn to God's Word for guidance regarding daily life and decisions.

Set an Example of Reading Scripture, and Teach Your Children to Spend Time in God's Word

You, however, continue in the things you have learned and become convinced of, knowing from whom you have learned them, and that from childhood you have known the sacred writings which are able to give you the wisdom that leads to salvation through faith which is in Christ Jesus. All Scripture is inspired by God and profitable for teaching, for reproof, for correction, for training in righteousness.
(2 Timothy 3:14-16)

---

[28]Craig L. Blomberg, *The New American Commentary: Matthew* (Nashville, TN: Broadman Press, 1992), 174.

Paul's letter to Timothy includes an affirmation that God's Word is "a training tool used by the Holy Spirit for salvation."[29] Therefore, if parents want to evangelize their children, the Bible is indispensable.

Children's Bibles

Even toddlers can learn that the Bible is a special book. They can repeat, "The Bible is God's Word," and understand that we treat it with respect and reverence.

Give your children, no matter their age, their own Bibles. For young preschoolers and even for older children, a Bible with realistic pictures will be best. Young preschoolers can flip through the pages of a Bible and tell you what they see. They can look for pictures that include water or animals or groups of people or even depictions of Jesus. Younger preschoolers and children need Bibles with sturdy covers and large print. Bible storybooks are nice, but make sure your children understand the difference between a small collection of stories and a complete copy of the Bible. Additionally, many Bible storybooks avoid paying for copyrights by paraphrasing God's Word or manipulating it in order to highlight a certain style of artwork, so make sure your Bible storybook contains an accurate rendering of Scripture.[30]

Family and Personal Devotions

Do not leave your child's experience with Scripture up to the "professionals" at your church. God has given the responsibility to parents to lead children spiritually. The role of the church is to come alongside parents and partner with them in bringing up their children in the ways of the Lord; parents are the ones who lay the foundation.

---

[29]Waylan Owens, "Preparing a Child's Heart to Respond to Christ," *The Alabama Baptist*, Vol. 175, no. 40, (2010), 9-16.
[30]For a list of recommended children's Bibles and Bible storybooks, see Appendix B.

Set aside time on a regular basis to look at God's Word as a family. Some families do this around meals or bedtimes. It does not have to be a full-blown worship service with a long sermon, special music, and an offertory. Depending on your children's ages, it might not last more than five minutes at a time. Just set apart some time that works for your family to read part of God's Word, make application of that Word to your lives, and pray, thanking God for His provision for every family member.[31]

Regarding parents' personal Scripture reading, many parents find it convenient and more efficient to read their Bibles while children are sleeping or otherwise occupied. Finding time for effective and meaningful time in God's Word is certainly important—just make sure your children know that your Bible does not only stay in the family car waiting for its weekly trip to church. Invite your children individually to join you on occasion or allow them to "catch" you reading God's Word. Younger children especially need to see you reading God's Word for it to register that you are actually doing what you are asking them to do.

Early readers can start picking out simple words as you read to them. This may take a little extra time, but many children are excited when they are learning to read. Letting them find words they can read from your family devotions will be special for them. As children are able to read more independently, there are numerous resources available through various Christian bookstores for boys and girls to have their own devotional guides. Again, just make sure the guides include daily interaction with Scripture and guidance for application and prayer related to the daily readings.

Scripture Memory

Memorizing Scripture is a healthy spiritual discipline to adopt, particularly at an early age. Psalm 119:9 says young men keep their ways pure by living according to God's Word, and in verse 11, the psalmist adds, "Your word I have treasured in my heart,

---

[31]For more on the how and why of family worship, see chapter 3 of this volume.

that I may not sin against You." This speaks to the importance of memorizing God's Word in order to live a holy life.

If your children attend a weekly Bible study or other program where Scripture memory is encouraged, consider selecting one of those passages for a monthly family Scripture memory focus from time to time. That way, your children will have a higher likelihood of successfully memorizing a certain passage.

Not all children memorize Scripture at the same rate. Oftentimes, using Scripture set to music is helpful for children and adults alike. The words are repeated and are usually set to catchy tunes so that memorizing longer passages becomes enjoyable and easy.

Another approach to consider is selecting genres of Scripture that pique your child's interests. If your child enjoys poetry or music, start with some verses from Psalms. If your child enjoys riddles, some of the Proverbs are especially interesting. If your child enjoys hunting or action stories, select a Bible passage that is packed with action and drama, then decide together which verse or verses from the passage will be most helpful and meaningful to your child's life for him to memorize. There will be some Scriptures that do not necessarily match up with your child's natural interests—for example, "Children, obey your parents in the Lord, for this is right" (Ephesians 6:1)—but you can weave those into the weekly or monthly memory rotation, and that will provide an opportunity to discuss how to apply all of Scripture to daily life.

Try to discover what method and what time of day works best for each child in your care. Verses—written by hand by each child who is able—taped to a bathroom mirror or printed on a chalkboard in a child's room work well for some children, whereas typed-out verses waiting in a special box at the dinner table work well for others. Letting your children take turns designing your family computer's screen saver with a favorite verse will be interesting to some, whereas letting them pick out different colored highlighters to use in their Bibles will work better for others. If you involve your children in selecting various methods as well as some of the verses, their interest will last longer than if you require everyone to learn the same verse in the same way all the time.

Review previously learned verses from time to time and make an effort to prompt recollection of certain verses when you see an immediate application or example of Scripture as you drive to run errands or walk to school. Listen to Christian music in the car or at home. CDs and videos that provide word-for-word Scripture set to catchy tunes are widely available. Many young families enjoy playing and singing along as a family. Children learn through repetition, and music is a fun and helpful way through which to learn Scripture together as a family.

Using a Catechism for Children

A catechism is a set of questions and answers used to teach spiritual principles and doctrines. Tom Nettles notes, "When it has a comprehensive scriptural orientation and is organized logically, a catechism can enhance understanding and give immense help in grasping the sense of Scripture."[32]

Ed Gravely, associate professor of Christian studies at Charleston Southern University, has modified Spurgeon's *Catechism for Children*, and it is a helpful and thorough catechism that parents can use "to present true contextual understanding of biblical revelation"[33] to their older preschoolers and children of all ages.[34]

In using the catechism, a parent reads each question and teaches the answer to the children. After a child is able to answer correctly, the parent can move on to the next question and answer. When the second question-and-answer set is complete, the parent can go back and ask question one, followed by question two, then add another question-and-answer set until he/she is able to work through the entire set of questions and answers.

---

[32]Tom J. Nettles, *Teaching Truth, Training Hearts: The Study of Catechisms in Baptist Life* (Amityville, NY: Calvary Press Publishing, 1998), 32.
[33]Ibid.
[34]A copy of this modified catechism can be found in Appendix C.

At first glance, this appears to be a bit daunting, but after you spend time discussing the answers and going over the question-and-answer pairings, it becomes easier and gives your children not only a sense of accomplishment but also a strong foundation for a Christian worldview as well as a useful tool to help share the Gospel with others.

Set an Example of Reliance on God and Teach Your Children to Pray

Pray without ceasing.
(1 Thessalonians 5:17)

While not a call to 24/7 prayer (though some parents may smile through gritted teeth that this is needed for a particularly precocious child), here Paul intends for believers to maintain a consistent practice of praying about every aspect of life. Praying continually is one command that many parents affirm as a necessity for parental survival. But beyond praying for mere parental survival, it is important to remember to pray *for* and *with* your children. Even before a child is born, parents can begin to pray for their child's spiritual growth and for opportunities to share Christ through example and conversation.

If prayer had training wheels, it would surely be "bow your head and close your eyes." Before children turn 1 year old, they are able to mimic your praying hands. Eventually, children who observe parents praying at bedtime or meals will try to say or shout "amen" when you have concluded your prayer. Even before your children understand why or what you are praying about, they will learn that you are doing something special, they will hear you mention God with reverent tones of gratitude or intercession, and they will know it is something they can do themselves one day. You are setting an example for a healthy spiritual habit that is important and efficacious.

Rick Osborne, in his thorough and excellent treatment of prayer with preschoolers and children, *Teaching Your Child How to Pray,* encourages parents to help their children grow from being nurtured and "taken" to the presence of God to being more personally involved in discussing what they would like to pray about.[35] As children are able to provide input and direction for their personal prayers, they should start to understand "the place and purpose of prayer. They should begin to understand that prayer is for every day, it's important for all of life, and it's God's way of letting them get to know Him and receive His help and care."[36]

Osborne suggests five truths for your children to learn primarily between the ages of 4 and 6:

- God hears us when we pray.
- God wants to be our friend.
- God wants us to talk to Him every day about everything we're thinking about and need.
- Prayer is great and really important.
- God wants us to pray for others.[37]

By age 7, Osborne notes that children should be saying their own prayers, and parents can stand by for assistance or coaching. Take turns praying together and talk about your children's day to help discover some topics for your children's prayers.[38]

Around age 9 or 10, "children should be learning to pray and be submitting themselves and their behavior to God."[39] Encourage your children in their prayer lives and talk with them about your prayer life, answered prayers, or people for whom you are praying.

Regardless of age or what direction their prayers take, "approach prayer with excitement, ... use variety, ... and encourage [your children in their] progress."[40] For many people, the prayer of

[35]Rick Osborne, *Teaching Your Child How to Pray* (Chicago, IL: Moody Press, 2000), 140-141.
[36]Ibid., 142.
[37]Ibid., 143.
[38]Ibid.
[39]Ibid.
[40]Ibid., 74-75.

salvation is their first real prayer or cry to God. Help your children develop an ongoing relationship with God and a habit of talking about anything and everything with God so that one day, when they are ready to receive Christ as Savior, it will be a deepening and strengthening of a relationship rather than an introduction.

Many parents agree that it is important to pray for their children. But it is also important that your children know you are praying for them. Mention them by name in your bedtime or mealtime prayers. Ask them about what they might like for you to pray for or with them, and then let them know you have followed up and prayed about their concerns.

Make the Most of Holidays

Christmas and Easter are obvious holidays at which times parents can share the true story of Christ. You can be sure children will hear plenty about the secular components of these special days while they are at school, in the mall, or from neighborhood friends and television. While regular church attendance is certainly beneficial, it is in the home that your child will have the most time for individual conversations, story reading, and even play related to the true meaning of Christmas and Easter.

Develop traditions in your home that are centered on the biblical texts. You may want to purchase a nativity set that is suitable for pretend play for your preschooler or younger child. Children of all ages can help create or display nativity sets on their own. A quick visit to Pinterest will provide you with ample biblical activities and crafts for your children.

There are certainly many time-honored traditions during the holidays, but do not let the busyness of the season pass you by without making a plan to have direct and meaningful conversations and activities with your children that reinforce the good news that God sent His son to be the Savior of the world. Many families set aside a special time during their Christmas and Easter gatherings to read the biblical text together. Family members can take turns reading from Scripture and praying together a prayer of thanksgiving for God's great gift to all people.

Other holidays also offer opportunities to discuss God's plan for daily living. Valentine's Day, Mother's Day, Father's Day, Veteran's Day, Memorial Day, Thanksgiving—all of these can be tied in various ways to what the Bible says about how we love and care for one another. You can learn a special verse about loving others or recount the story from Mark 2:3-5 about how four men went to great lengths to take a paralytic man to Jesus by lowering him through the roof of a crowded building. You will not be looking for a way to rationalize national holidays as biblical; rather, you will take the general theme or idea of the holiday and ask, "What does the Bible have to say about such ideas?" What does the Bible say about caring for parents, honoring elders, giving thanks to God, and showing love to others?

Share Your Personal Testimony and Give a Clear Gospel Presentation to Your Children

All of the aforementioned strategies and activities work well for both laying a foundation of biblical knowledge and practices for children as well as for strengthening a child's personal relationship with Christ. At some point along the way, however, children will need to make their own decisions about whether they will accept Christ as their personal Savior. Your children may come to you with questions about something they read in the Bible or heard at home or at church. Or, you may feel the prompting of the Holy Spirit to give a clear Gospel presentation to your children. However the conversation develops, you will need to be ready to respond in a clear way that your children will understand.

As previously noted, there are no junior rules for children to accept Christ. Christians at any age must first understand that they are sinners in need of forgiveness and then understand that Christ alone was able to take the punishment for our sins by dying on the cross. A good exercise for parents wanting to share the Gospel with their children is to "translate" their personal testimonies in such a way that communicates to children. This will help your children understand that you have already made a commitment to what you are asking or helping them to do.

Take a few minutes and write out a brief personal testimony including what your life was like before you became a Christian and how you realized you needed a Savior, how you became a Christian, and what your life has been like since you accepted Christ. Then, take a good look at every word and make changes to various vocabulary words so that what you are saying is communicated at your child's level.

For example, if you mention, "I realized I was lost," consider changing that to something like, "I understood that I was not trusting Jesus to be in charge of my life and help me follow Him every day." Try to think of substitutes for "churchy" words or words that are difficult for children to understand. Practice saying your children's edition of your testimony to your spouse or a friend and see if it still communicates what you want to say but in a kid-friendly way.

When you are ready to continue a conversation with your children about accepting Christ, try to ascertain, if you have not already, if they understand what sin is and if they see themselves as sinners. Many times, boys and girls know what sin is but are not ready to admit that they themselves are sinners. They might be ready to admit that their parents or siblings are sinners, but they do not recognize that in themselves.

Take time to define and talk about sin. Simply ask your children if they can give you an example of sin, then follow that up with asking if they can name any sins they have done. That will help you know if you are ready to move on to the next step, which is seeing if your children understand what God did about our sin.

A few simple ways to explain sin to children are: "Sin is anything we think, say, or do that is displeasing to God"; or, "Sin is when we do things *our* way instead of *God's* way." Even if a child is not willing to admit he is a sinner, you can go ahead and share

Romans 3:23, "For all have sinned and fall short of the glory of God." ALL have sinned, and that includes your children, their parents, their teachers, their pastor … EVERYONE. If, at this point, you do not feel your children are ready to accept Christ, go ahead and finish the Gospel presentation, then pray that God will help your children know when it is time to accept Christ as their personal Savior.

When using Scripture to help present the Gospel, it is good to read or quote the text straight from the Bible, then follow it up with any clarification that is needed for your children. For example, after you have established that your children are sinners, then move on to what the Bible teaches about the consequences of sin. Romans 6:23 declares, "For the wages of sin is death, but the free gift of God is eternal life in Christ Jesus our Lord." It is helpful to break that verse down into two parts for children—what our sin deserves, followed by what God did about that.

"Wages" is another word that is difficult for young children to understand. If you explain that every Friday, Mrs. Petersen receives a check for the hard work she does as a nurse at the children's hospital (or name a relative or family friend whom your children will know), then those are her wages. Wages are what she deserves for what she did. In the same way, our sin deserves to be punished. This does not mean that we are going to physically die every time we sin, but if we do not accept God's gift, then we will be separated from Him after we die.

God's gift to us is that He sent His son, Jesus, to die on the cross and take the punishment we deserve for our sins. If we accept His gift, then we can have a relationship with Jesus now as well as after we die a physical death.

Accepting God's gift of Jesus sounds confusing to some young children. They cannot just unwrap it like a Christmas present and put it in their pockets to take home. The special way to accept God's gift is by praying to God and admitting one's sin, believing that Jesus is God's son who died on the cross to take the punishment for our sins, and then asking Jesus to be in charge of your life.

After you present the Gospel directly to your children, if they are not ready, then go ahead and pray with them before closing your time together. Ask your children what they would like to pray about, then pray about that together. Include in your prayer thanksgiving to God for sending His son Jesus to die for our sins and a request that God help your children know when it is time for them to ask Jesus to be in charge of their lives. It is important to keep the conversation pressure-free and for the children to understand that accepting Christ as Savior is something only they can do for themselves.

Some children come to the salvation conversation because of their questions about or desire to be baptized. A useful way to explain baptism to children is to illustrate how baptism is a picture with your body about what you believe in your heart and mind. When people see someone being baptized, they know that he believes that Jesus died on the cross for his sins, was buried, and rose again. (It is helpful at this point to illustrate baptism and Jesus' death, burial, and resurrection with hand motions showing the similarity between the two events.) Sometimes, children are simply curious about what it means and are not necessarily ready to accept Christ, but other times, the Holy Spirit will use that conversation to help a child gain a greater understanding about what God did for us through Christ Jesus.

Conclusion

In the book of Matthew, children are recorded shouting, "Hosanna to the Son of David" after Jesus drives the money-changers out of the temple (Matthew 21:15). Elsewhere, Christ praises the Father for revealing His truths "to little children" (Matthew 11:25, NIV).

Many times in Scripture, the parent/child relationship is addressed, but most frequently, the Word instructs and informs thoughts, attitudes, and behaviors of Christ-followers; and parents are expected to rear their children in such a way as to pass along, encourage, and expect a godly lifestyle from their children.

In so doing, it is important and effective for parents not only to set examples of devotion and submission to Christ's commands but also to plan and prepare intentionally for ways that children in their care can learn and practice spiritual disciplines. In addition to laying a strong and proper foundation for following Christ, parents must be intentional and direct in sharing with their children how to begin and grow in their own personal relationships with Christ.

CHAPTER 3

SPIRITUAL FORMATION
THROUGH FAMILY WORSHIP:
THE HEART OF THE MATTER

By Malcolm and Karen Yarnell

Maybe you have faced one of the following difficult situations in your family: A child consistently and willfully misbehaves after he perceives that a parent is favoring another child; a man and his wife have difficulties in their intimate relations with one another; an in-law dominates the family's discussions in a negative way.

We could delve further into each of these crises and define the root causes from different perspectives. Is the child displaying rebellion because of an improper diet, a hidden and unresolved sin, or a genuine grievance against a sibling? Is the marriage in trouble because of a lack of trust from previous sexual habits, a kink in the finances, or a stressful situation at work? Is the in-law aware of, yet oblivious to, his undue demands, crying out for genuine spiritual assistance, or suffering from an undetected sickness?

While the critical problems that we face in our personal and family lives may have multiple symptoms—in the realm of the physical body, of the social context, or of any number of extraneous conditions, real or perceived—there is really one place where it all comes together. The root issue for the human being is not in the constriction of finances, the behavior of siblings or spouses, or the illness of the human body. These are all important areas that must necessarily be addressed in the proper time and way, but they are not at the heart of the matter. Rather, the root issue in every human life is the condition of the human heart as it exists before God.

"Man looks at the outward appearance, but the Lord looks at the heart" (1 Samuel 16:7). At the heart of the matter *is* the matter of the heart. The human heart must receive God's healing touch in order for the other difficulties in one's personal, family, and social life to be brought to a true solution.

But how is the heart—your heart and your loved one's heart—to be healed? What does the healthy heart look like? What brings about healing? Who can administer the restorative balm the wounded heart requires? And how can this healing formula be applied to the human heart?

When we get honest and see the problems in our own homes, we want to see things made well. We want to see healing, but who can do it, and how can they do it? Through family worship, God's presence is recognized in the home, for in the reading of His Word and the movement of His Spirit, hearts are transformed.

From Brokenness to Healing

The path to healing begins with an understanding of our need for God. First, let it be clear from the beginning that every human heart needs healing. Every heart has been corrupted by sin—your own heart is broken in its relationship with God; your spouse's heart is broken; and your child's heart is broken. "The heart is more deceitful than all else" (Jeremiah 17:9a). The truth is that the human heart—the inner core of our mind, emotions, and will—is beyond self-repair. It is "desperately sick; who can understand it?" (Jeremiah 17:9b).

Second, while every heart is irreparably broken beyond our ability even to understand, God does understand the human heart. "I, the Lord, search the heart, I test the mind..." (Jeremiah 17:10a). At one point, the apostle Paul, a very godly, wise, and inspired apostle, admitted that even he was not proficient at properly judging himself. We are incapable of getting at the core problem in our own lives, much less anybody else's (1 Corinthians 4:2-3). But God is capable of judging the heart (Psalm 139:23), and He indeed judges the heart (Jeremiah 17:10b). Our hearts are broken with sin, and God looks on the heart to judge it. However, these truths need not bring us to despair.

The third truth is good news. God hears the prayers of people who perceive that their hearts are deformed; He can and will create in them a new heart. Why would God do this? Because God loves us, and He wants to be present with us, beginning in our hearts, forever. The Shema, the greatest commandment, declares, "You shall love the Lord your God with all your heart..." (Deuteronomy 6:5). We cannot fulfill this command on our own, but God can do it within us, and He wants to do it for us. "I will give you a new heart" (Ezekiel 36:26).

But how does God do this? God the Father transforms human hearts by His Word and by His Spirit. This third and very beautiful truth requires a bit more discussion.

The God We Worship: The Father, the Word, and the Spirit

God works upon our human hearts in a threefold way. God the Father works upon human hearts externally by His Word, internally by His Spirit, and for the purpose of restoring human beings to a right relationship with Him.

First, God works in our hearts through external or outward means, specifically through His Word. God works through other people as instruments when one person proclaims His Word to another. The Word of God comes through the lips of one person into the ears of another person, where God begins to work on the human heart (Romans 10:6-17).

The greatest hymn regarding the correlation of the Word of God with the heart of man is found in Psalm 119. Listen to that psalm's poetic description of how God's Word works to bring the human heart into communion with God:

How can a young man keep his way pure?
 By keeping it according to Your word.
With all my heart I have sought You;
 Do not let me wander from your commandments.
Your word I have treasured in my heart,
 That I may not sin against You. (Psalm 119:9-11)

Consider also Jeremiah's prophecy: "I will put My law within them and on their heart I will write it" (Jeremiah 31:33b). The promised new covenant was fulfilled in Jesus Christ, and His salvation becomes a person's own possession when the Gospel of the Word of God is proclaimed, heard, and believed in the heart (Romans 10:9).

The Gospel is the central, saving message of the Bible about the death of Christ for our sins and His resurrection, so that those who believe in Him may be declared right with God. "If you confess with your mouth Jesus as Lord, and believe in your heart that God raised Him from the dead, you will be saved; for with the heart a person believes, resulting in righteousness, and with the mouth he confesses, resulting in salvation" (Romans 10:9-10). Dear reader, if you have not believed in the Gospel and confessed that Jesus is God and your Lord, then we beg of you, please do so now!

Second, God also works through internal or mysterious means, directly and immediately upon the human heart. This work is identified with the sovereign movement of the Holy Spirit in the human heart. Remember David's prophetic prayer: "Create in me a clean heart, O God, and renew a steadfast spirit within me. Do not cast me away from your presence or take your Holy Spirit from me" (Psalm 51:10-11). Also, remember Ezekiel's moving prophecy about the resurrecting power of the Holy Spirit: "I will give you a new heart and put a new spirit within you; and I will remove the heart of stone from your flesh and give you a heart of flesh. I will put my Spirit within you and cause you to walk in my statutes, and you will be careful to observe my ordinances" (Ezekiel 36:26-27).

Third, God the Father works through His Word in His Spirit in order to bring us a new heart capable of living with Him in an intimate and eternal relationship. The saving work of God the Trinity upon humanity is always united—the Word and the Spirit work together to bring everyone into the presence of the Father (Ephesians 2:18).

Look again at the prophesies by Jeremiah and Ezekiel mentioned above and note what God does next. In Jeremiah, God promises to bring His Word into human hearts so that people might know Him intimately. Then, He says, "I will be their God, and they shall be my people" (Jeremiah 31:33c). In Ezekiel, God promises to work in our hearts through His Spirit so that we can live with Him forever. And then, He says, "You will be my people, and I will be your God" (Ezekiel 36:28b). God the Father sends forth His Word and His Spirit into our hearts so that we might hear and believe and be brought into the Father's presence (Galatians 4:4-6; Ephesians 2:18).

We have seen our need for God to change our hearts, and we have discussed how God works to change our hearts, but now let us look at family worship as a means for God to work in the spiritual formation of the family.

Why Is Family Worship a Priority?

God wants us to come into His presence in His Spirit through His Word. But why is family worship a priority? Why is family worship an important instrument for transforming the human heart so that we can know God intimately?

In Paul's letter to the Colossians, Christ is exalted as the true knowledge and the source of all wisdom. The insights found in worldly wisdom, psychology, and religious ritual are opposed to the true knowledge found in Christ. The last two chapters of the book of Colossians describe a community of believers living in

Christ. We find the Word of Christ spoken by the filling of the Spirit in thankfulness to the Father:

> Let the word of Christ richly dwell within you, with all wisdom teaching and admonishing one another with psalms and hymns and spiritual songs, singing with thankfulness in your hearts to God. Whatever you do in word or deed, do all in the name of the Lord Jesus, giving thanks through Him to God the Father. (Colossians 3:16-17)

This admonition of worship from the letter to the Colossians is mirrored in the letter from Paul to the Ephesians with a similar admonition to gather in worship:

> So then do not be foolish, but understand what the will of the Lord is. And do not get drunk with wine, for that is dissipation, but be filled with the Spirit, speaking to one another in psalms and hymns and spiritual songs, singing and making melody with your heart to the Lord; always giving thanks for all things in the name of our Lord Jesus Christ to God, even the Father; and be subject to one another in the fear of Christ. (Ephesians 5:17-21)

What is extremely interesting here is that both of these passages concern the gathering of believers for worship in the presence of the Father in Word and Spirit, and both of these passages immediately precede the instructions for the family, commonly called the household codes. In fact, Ephesians 5:22, which begins discussing the relationship of the wife to her husband, relies on the verb from verse 21. From this, it is evident that, for the apostle Paul, family worship and family structure are inextricably interconnected.

Some assume that family worship is conducted adequately in the worship of the local church. But is family worship only to be found in the gathering of the local church on Sunday morning? While corporate worship in the local church is vitally important for every Christian and every Christian family and should not be neglected, congregational worship cannot replace the need for worship in the home. In fact, the Lord instructed the children of Israel through Moses that God's Word was to be taught continually in the home:

> These words, which I am commanding you today, shall be on your heart. You shall teach them diligently to your sons and shall talk of them when you sit in your house and when you walk by the way and when you lie down and when you rise up. (Deuteronomy 6:6-7)

Family worship is simply an act of obedience to the command of the Lord. The consistent practice of joining together in the presence of God transforms the family (Romans 12:2). A family that finds its daily, moment-by-moment direction from God's Word has an identity in God. We are united in the worship of the One who guides and instructs us. He is sufficient to meet our needs in every circumstance.

The instruction given by Moses in Deuteronomy 6 does not promise a psychological quick fix for problems, nor does it command a ritual to be followed, but it calls the family to share all of life in the presence of God so that the following generations will fear the Lord and know His goodness and blessing (Deuteronomy 6:24).

I See the Importance of Family Worship, So Now What?

Most Christian adults agree wholeheartedly that the family should be engaged in regular worship in the home. But there is more often than not a stumbling block that appears when actually considering how to start and continue family worship. Please allow us to share a few ideas as to how the Lord might lead you to guide your family in worship.

Being faithful to God's Word, the leader of the family should embrace the freedom that God gives in shaping the practice of worship in your family. We would strongly encourage you not to build up unrealistic expectations; family worship often falters because we embrace unnecessary ideas about what must happen for family worship to occur.

The basic necessities of family worship consist of five simple things: a time, a place, the family, the Bible, and prayer.

A Time

As for time, we have learned over the years that a time in the evening, usually immediately after the family meal or immediately before bedtime preparation, is best. (We have chosen the mornings for our own personal Bible study and prayer times.) We encourage the parents to discuss shortly beforehand regarding the proper time and place for family worship and then inform the children. Sometimes, the children will happily remind us that we need to have "Family Bible Time."

It is important to be intentional about setting specific days and times for family worship, but not to be rigid or feel defeated when unexpected interruptions occur. We have found that Sundays and Wednesdays, due to church-based acts of worship, are best to forego. Most other days should be taken for granted as opportune for family worship. It is important to be flexible on the one hand but to be intentional to build a habit on the other hand.

Each family's schedule will determine the best time for worship. One family we know, due to the father's job situation, had worship at 5:30 in the morning, since this was the only time they could all be together. They may have struggled to stay awake at times, but the family was faithful to worship together.

A Place

We have found ourselves gathering as a family for worship all over the family home and, when traveling, in the car or hotel room or at a scenic but conveniently peaceful spot. In preparing the place for family worship, make sure there is room for every person either to stand or sit. Also, please be careful to turn off or turn away all distractions. If your family has the television, radio, or the internet progressing anywhere in the room, please change those devices so that they do not become instruments that disturb what God is doing in the midst of the family. Everyone's personal communication devices should be turned off entirely or at least silenced, including any and all forms of external notification. From a positive perspective, if a call or message is missed, it becomes a great opportunity to share the Gospel with the sender.

The Family

Everyone who is a part of the family and is available physically at family worship time should be invited to participate. While parents must be judicious about how the youngest children are doing, we have found that it is best to include even the babies. Though they can sometimes be rambunctious, young children learn quickly the importance of this family time. Our children have come to treasure these times of family worship; they see their parents read Scripture, discuss their own interpretations of Scripture, wrestle with crises, and learn that God answers prayer. The purpose of family worship is to bring the family before God Himself, so it is necessary for everybody to be involved, no matter the difficulties or fidgeting. If friends and extended family are present, then we invite them to participate, as well.

The Bible

As mentioned above, our children have come to call our family worship event "Family Bible Time," because the Bible is at the center of worship. Through Scripture, God speaks to us, communicates with us; the Word of God acts on us, piercing, dividing, and discerning the thoughts and intentions of the heart (Hebrews 4:12). The Bible is the means by which God has chosen to speak to and transform human hearts. The first part of communion with God is to hear God speak, and God speaks through Scripture. (The second part of communion with God is for us to speak to God, about which we discuss more below.)

As the father, who is responsible for the spiritual welfare of his wife and children, Malcolm takes the Bible in hand to read. Once everybody is somewhat settled, sometimes after Karen has encouraged respectful silence on the part of the children, Malcolm simply reads a text out of the Bible. It may be from Genesis or Revelation; it may be a psalm or an episode in the life of Jesus Christ; it may be one verse or a whole chapter. The point is not so much that a particular reading system is followed—though we like to move around and mix things up—but that the Bible is read.

The point is not to have a law-bound approach to reading the Bible, but simply to hear God's Word. God's Word has power to change lives on its own; simply read the Bible and let God work. Over time, you will be amazed at what God will do through His Word.

We have learned through the years that memorizing Scripture is as important for our own hearts as it is for our children's spiritual, emotional, and mental development. The whole family first committed to memory some basic Bible passages, such as John 3:16 and the Lord's Prayer, as well as the evangelistic passages in the Romans Road.

There are other venues we use for encouraging Scripture memory. For instance, Karen consistently brings the school-age children together each morning to read Scripture, hear a report from the mission field, pray, and memorize one passage every week. Malcolm communicates daily personal Bible readings and devotional thoughts to our sons and many of their friends each morning by group text. Moreover, we have required all of our children to enroll in our church's Bible Drill activity, which is focused on memorizing important Scriptural passages. Finally, we have come under conviction to memorize whole books of the Bible, and we are both excited and intimidated to do so.

Along with the external guidance from the Word of God, parents must also be sensitive to internal guidance from the Holy Spirit. Each family Bible time is unique. Sometimes, we can go for half an hour or longer; at other times, we gather only for five minutes. Typically, our family worship takes about fifteen minutes.

Sometimes, Dad simply reads the passage without commentary. At other times, Dad or Mom or one of the older children will share something that they have learned from their own study.

Sometimes, one of the younger children will raise her hand to ask a question. Perhaps an answer is possible, or perhaps an answer must be delayed for further study. The parents, like the children, are always growing in the Word, so it is okay to say, "I don't know. Let's ask God to show us. Let Dad and Mom study that some more."

Prayer

If communion with God requires that we hear from God, it also requires that God hear from us. The two most important activities in family worship are, therefore, reading the Bible and praying to God. While singing and theological reflection are often necessary and proper in family worship, Bible reading and prayer are non-negotiable necessities. Prayer involves opening our hearts to God and to one another and pouring everything out to Him. In content, prayer should include both confession and praise as well as petition. Prayer need not be complex nor extended, but it does need to come from the heart.

What do we confess? We must regularly confess to God the truths about who He is and who we are, and about our need for forgiveness and provision from Him.

First, confession includes stating what we believe about God. This may entail a simple reaffirmation of some basic truth about God and what He has created. Or, it may include, as many families have found helpful, the regular use of an orthodox creed or a catechism appropriate to the age-level of the younger children. While some families are adamant that a catechism must be used, we have found that a catechism is an aid, not a necessity. Scripture is a necessity.

Second, confession also includes stating where we stand personally with God. Sometimes, God leads one of us to confess a sin with which we have been struggling. Do not be afraid to admit your own weaknesses, for the children learn to confess sin to God and receive forgiveness through seeing the authentic repentance and gracious redemption of their parents. Be careful in doing this, remembering where your children are in their own psychological, social, and sexual development. Discussions concerning important moral or behavioral issues the family faces in church and society are often part of the discussion and prayer time.

In addition to confessing God and our relationship to God, prayer must involve praise. An important part of prayer is praising God for the incredible provisions He has made in the lives of one or more family members. Praise is often expressed best in song; psalms, hymns, and spiritual songs include both praise and confession. Moreover, singing during worship includes not only words directed toward God but also words spoken to one another.

Karen will often lead us in song, sometimes using the piano to lead our voices. Years ago, we bought each family member *The Baptist Hymnal* with his or her name embossed on it. If we do not sing a simple chorus, she will lead us in singing one of the old hymns, which contain important doctrinal statements. The internet is another useful resource for Christian music. Sometimes, we do not sing, although the Holy Spirit often uses musical recitation to incline the heart toward God.

This time of prayer is where the family has the opportunity to petition God concerning their needs and the needs of others. The salvation of a neighbor, healing for a loved one, or help with a school assignment may be voiced in the family prayer. No concern is too small and no situation too grim to be excluded from prayer. God's goodness and tender compassion are taught through the lifting up of family concerns in prayer to the Lord. As the family sees God answer prayer, faith grows in the hearts of all.

A Note for Special Circumstances

Your family situation may not consist of two believing parents with children. God still desires for you to worship Him. If you are a single parent or married to an unbelieving spouse, then you can still worship with your children. Your testimony to the Lord will be a powerful witness to your children, even if you do not have a spouse to support you. If you are a married couple but do not have children, or children living in the home, make a commitment to worship as a couple. If you are single, find others to meet in small groups or in a one-on-one setting for a time of worship on a consistent basis.

Our Heart's Desire

We pray you will be blessed, like we have been blessed, when you make family worship a regular part of your lives together. Family worship prepares our hearts to hear from God in the Word and to confess and praise Him in the Spirit. In family worship, we come into the blessed presence of God through Christ Jesus in the Holy Spirit. That is the most important thing you can ever give your family, and it only takes a little bit of time, though it takes all of your heart.

Practical Suggestions
1. Begin with a prayer of commitment, asking the Lord to make family worship a priority for your family. It is only through the power of God's Spirit that we are able to be consistent in His Word.
2. Speak to the other members about family worship. Explain the importance of reading God's Word together.

3. Do not be discouraged. Some of the times together will be wonderful. Some of the times together may cause you to question why you are even trying to have family worship. Remember, we obey because God has commanded us, not because we see the results we expect.

4. Remember that the children are being trained. They will not always see the importance of this time or know exactly how to behave. In love, train them to listen to God's Word.

5. Give each family member opportunities to contribute to the worship time. Examples of tasks are: reading the passage; praying; leading in a song; finding or creating artwork that expresses a biblical truth; sharing what God has taught them in personal time with God or in church.

6. Sometimes, on special occasions, our children will draw an order of worship and assign tasks for each family member.

7. Always remember to praise God for the blessings He constantly gives you and your family.

CHAPTER 4

RAISING MEN IN A CULTURE OF BOYS

By Dean Nichols

J.M. Barrie's well-known book entitled *Peter Pan; or, The Boy Who Wouldn't Grow Up* is almost a story of our time. We are living in a time where, if a young boy grows up to become a man in any sense of the word, it is almost by accident. Our culture, our education system, and, to some extent, even our churches are contributing to this disaster of Peter Pan and his band of lost boys, whose only aspiration in life is to live in a world away from reality.

Toward the end of the fairy tale, Wendy decides she needs to leave Neverland to return home with her younger brothers. Peter Pan goes ahead of her and alters the window of Wendy's room to make Wendy think that her mother has forgotten her. But then Peter sees Wendy's mother, Mrs. Darling, and the condition she is in because of her missing daughter. So, Peter brings Wendy home and meets Mrs. Darling, who adopts the lost boys and offers to adopt Peter Pan as well. But Peter refuses because he is scared that they will "catch him and make him a man."

So we, too, live in a society that is scared to let "men be men." I could go into a long diatribe of how we got here, but that would serve no purpose at this time. I would, however, like to share how we can get back to having men be men.

Manhood under Attack

I lost both of my parents when I was 10 years old. My father died of a heart attack, and a few months later, my mother was killed in a car accident. This resulted in my being raised by my grandparents. I guess you could say I was raised "old school."

There were two sayings that I heard consistently from my grandparents as I was growing up. Inevitably, as I was walking out the door, one of them would shout out to me, "Dean, remember whose child you are." They had lived in that small Texas community for years and did not want their name tarnished by some foolish act on my part. It was important to them that I not hurt the family honor or the family name. The other saying I heard a lot was, "Just be a man!" In the back of my mind, those words of encouragement still ring out to me: "Be a man!"

In so many ways, our culture has assaulted the role of men and the notion of being masculine. It is almost something that many want men to be ashamed of. Society says you can proudly be female, transgender, or same-sex attracted, and those things are to be celebrated; but you cannot celebrate just being a man. Hopefully, this will soon change and people will wake up to see where that has taken us—no place good, that's for sure!

Being raised "old school," I was influenced by the generation that is now called the "greatest generation." My grandparents did not believe in a stage called "adolescence." You were either a child or you were a man; maybe a young man but, nonetheless, a man.

A great disservice was done to manhood by creating the idea of adolescence. It is a stage of "no man's land," pun fully intended. They are not children, but they are not yet adults either, resulting in a "get out of jail free" card (and kids are smart enough to figure this out). It has worked against society, and it has worked against the child caught in this false stage of adolescence as well. Its results can be seen in our school system and especially in our criminal justice system, where juveniles can commit all sorts of crimes and yet have these crimes expunged from their record when they turn 18.

That is just not how I was raised. I was expected to act like an adult, specifically a male adult—a man. From a very young age, my grandparents referred to me as a man—sometimes a young man, but a man. That did something for me. It made me rise to the occasion. I was not allowed to be what Proverbs would call "foolish."

Wisdom from Proverbs

One of the terms that Proverbs uses in describing foolish behavior is "naïve." This implies that the individual is young and has not yet had the experiences of life to learn many of life's imperative lessons. I recall my former pastor, John Morgan of Sagemont Church in Houston, Texas, often saying, "A smart man learns from his mistakes, but a wise man learns from someone else's mistakes." One of the purposes of Proverbs is to help young men learn from other men's mistakes.

I have 65 years of life experiences, including raising nine children. Given the chance to do some things differently, I would concentrate on the book of Proverbs as a teaching tool for training my children and myself in the affairs of this life. I would begin with Proverbs 1:7—"The fear of the Lord is the beginning of knowledge"—because that has to be the beginning place if anything is to make sense at all in the world in which we live. Just as it is stated in Genesis 1:1—"In the beginning God..."—so we, too, must begin with God.

One of the greatest men in the Bible was King David. He was, among many things, a man's man. He was a musician, poet, statesman, shepherd, warrior, and king, but above all things, he was "a man after God's own heart" (Acts 13:22). As this man lay on his deathbed, he called for his son Solomon, and in the last recorded words from King David, we hear him say to his son, "I am going the way of all the earth. Be strong, therefore, and show yourself a man" (1 Kings 2:2). He further directed his son to "keep the charge of the Lord your God, to walk in His ways, to keep His statutes, His commandments, His ordinances, and His testimonies" (1 Kings 2:3). David wanted his son to be a godly man.

What do you want *your* son to be? If you could only have a few words to describe him, what would they include? Rich? Handsome? Healthy? Wealthy? Successful? What the writer of Proverbs wanted most for his son was that he be wise in the things of God. For by raising his child to be wise, he knew that the child would have all that he needed in life and that the blessings of God would be upon him at the same time.

John Phillips, in his excellent commentary on Proverbs, tells the story of his time spent at Moody Bible Institute Correspondence School. He had agreed to be in charge of course development tests in order to evaluate the students' mastery of the material studied. He soon realized that before he could write the tests, he had to know what the material was.[41]

A good way for parents to familiarize themselves with the material they desire to share with their sons is to read one chapter in the book of Proverbs a day, the one that corresponds to the day's date. In other words, on the first of each month, read Proverbs 1, and on the second of each month, read Proverbs 2, and continue that practice until the end of the month. With 31 chapters in Proverbs, you will always have enough chapters for the month.

I also try to find something that I am looking for. That is, I will pick a topic or a word and mark it in my Bible each time I find it. For instance, I might pick the word "fool" and mark it each and every time it occurs in my reading that month.[42] My copy of Proverbs then becomes my own personal color-coded reference for each of those topics, and I can quickly find the verses for which I am looking by simply glancing through the pages. This has aided me in knowing and understanding the book of Proverbs.

---

[41]John Phillips, *Exploring Proverbs: An Expository Commentary* (Grand Rapids, MI: Kregel Publications, 2002), 19.

[42]I use colored pencils so as not to bleed through the pages.

Once you have become familiar with the book (or perhaps even while you are still familiarizing yourself with it), you can then share the Scriptural truths with your children. The daily reading of Proverbs around the breakfast table is an excellent way to saturate your children's minds with wisdom and can be used in your family's devotions.

I want to interact with Proverbs 1:2-6 as it relates to raising children and the parents' desire for their children. I believe that this text contains most of the information we need in order to have a better understanding of what we are to teach our sons. In Proverbs 1:2-6, the inspired Word of God tells us what the "material for life" is:

- To know wisdom and instruction – 1:2
- To discern the sayings of understanding – 1:2
- To receive instruction in wise behavior, righteousness, justice, and equity – 1:3
- To give prudence to the naive – 1: 4
- To give young men knowledge and discretion – 1:4
- To understand a proverb and a figure, the words of the wise and their riddles – 1:6

Proverbs provides the material that must be mastered for the tests that are sure to come in this life. I am mainly addressing men and their sons, but the wisdom found in Proverbs applies to your daughters as well.

The knowledge and wisdom that our children need to know have their start in the book of Proverbs and, ultimately, in the entire Bible. The wisdom we seek and strive to teach to our children is described in Job 28:12-28. Job concludes with his definition of wisdom: "Behold, the fear of the Lord, that is wisdom; and to depart from evil is understanding" (verse 28).

The word "instruction" in Proverbs 1:2-3 has a connotation of discipline and is sometimes even translated "chastisement." Proverbs 1:2-6 uses a combination of words to describe what the book will teach its readers. They will become skillful in handling all of life's situations and will be considered wise or smart by others.

The 31 chapters in the book of Proverbs contain the wisdom Christian parents should want to convey to their children in relation to being moral, upright individuals. I am amazed at how relevant this book is to every culture and generation. Proverbs 1 deals with gang violence, something we see most nights on the evening news. Imagine if the young people who end up in gangs had been given the type of knowledge and wisdom that Proverbs offers—perhaps it could have prevented their downfall.

In Proverbs 2, we see that this wisdom will protect you from the evil person (2:12-15) as well as the immoral woman (2:16-19). This kind of wisdom promises protection that only godly wisdom can provide. Challenge your son to memorize this and other chapters of Proverbs. Reward him generously when he accomplishes it. It will be one of the best investments you will ever make.

Proverbs addresses other topics such as work ethic, honesty, anger, money, friendships, fools, and foes. All of this wisdom is only beneficial for the individuals who seek after and apply it to their lives. Therefore, as Proverbs 2:2-4 instructs, let us incline our ear to wisdom, apply our hearts to understanding, cry out for discernment, seek wisdom as we would silver, and search for wisdom as we would for hidden treasures.

The Wise Man and the Fool

Two kinds of people are compared and contrasted in the book of Proverbs: the wise man and the foolish man. Consider some of the comparisons that Proverbs makes between these two kinds of people:

A wise man will hear and increase in learning (1:5; 9:9; 18:15); a foolish man despises wisdom and instruction (1:7).

A wise man will inherit honor (3:35);
    a foolish man will receive dishonor (3:35).

A wise man will receive correction (9:8; 15:31);
    a foolish man hates correction (9:8; 13:1; 15:12).

A wise man will make his parents glad (10:1; 15:20; 23:24);
    a foolish man will bring shame and grief to his parents (10:1; 15:20).

A wise man will listen to counsel (1:5; 12:15);
    a foolish man rejects counsel from others (12:15).

A wise man is cautious about things in life (14:16);
    a foolish man is arrogant and careless (14:16).

A wise man turns away from anger (29:8, 11);
    a foolish man is angry and expresses it (12:16; 29:8, 11).

A wise man will build his home (14:1);
    a foolish man will tear down his home (14:1).

A wise man will accept his father's discipline (13:1);
    a foolish man will not listen to rebuke (13:1).

I fully agree that children are a gift from the Lord, but if these children are not taught or do not accept the wisdom and knowledge of Proverbs and the rest of God's Word, then these "gifts" can bring shame and grief to their parents.[43] You have probably observed this in someone's family, if not your own.

If we desire for boys to become men, then we must teach them what it means to be a man. At what age do you expect a boy to become a man? 13? 18? 21? In the Jewish culture, it was 12. Proverbs does not recognize the stage of adolescence; one is either wise

---

[43]See Proverbs 10:1; 17:25; 29:15.

or naïve. Remember, the term "naïve," as used in Proverbs, implies that the individual is young and has not yet had the experiences of life to learn many of life's imperative lessons. He can learn from his own mistakes or from the mistakes of others. Proverbs encourages him to learn from other people's mistakes.

If the "naïve" or "simple" man refuses wisdom, then he progresses to the next step of foolishness—he becomes "a scoffer." According to Proverbs, there is some hope for the scoffer, though not much. To persist as a scoffer means one looks out only for himself; he does things his way; he trusts in his own heart and mind; he exalts himself.

At the end of this road, the scoffer arrives at his new condition—that of a fool. Proverbs gives no hope for the fool. A wise man follows God and His Word; a fool follows his own heart and desires.

We all make foolish choices sometimes, and our sons will as well. What we want to prevent, if we can, is a pattern of foolishness. We are called to teach, and they are called to learn. I love what Steve Farrar writes in his insightful book *King Me*:

> Fathers are to sons what blacksmiths are to swords. It is the job of the blacksmith not only to make a sword but also to maintain its edge of sharpness. It is the job of the father to keep his son sharp and save him from the dullness of foolishness. He gives his son that sharp edge through discipline.[44]

The process of making a sword or knife is an amazing one. If the craftsman makes it from scratch, he starts with a chunk of metal and heats it until it glows red. He then takes it out of the furnace and hits it with his hammer until it takes the shape that the craftsman desires. He must then treat the metal so that it does not break under stress.

[44]Steve Farrar, *King Me* (Chicago, IL: Moody Publishers, 2005), 96.

This is a make or break point in the process. If the knife takes the treatment, then all is well. If not, the blade is discarded, and the process is started over again. We do not want our sons to be like the one spoken of in Proverbs 24:10—"If you faint in the day of adversity, your strength is small" (NKJV). We must work with them until they develop the strength of character that will last through the trials of life. Then they will be a sword fit for the Master's use.

What If My Son is a Prodigal?

We started with Proverbs 1:7 and the fear of the Lord being the beginning of wisdom, but there is a second part to that verse. It says, "Fools despise wisdom and instruction."

This is one of the mysteries of this life that I honestly do not understand—how children from the same parents and the same home, raised in the same environment, can turn out so differently. One can be wise and the other, foolish.

Where does the child begin this process of becoming a fool, and how do you deal with it? I so wish I had some answers to this question.

You and I have seen this happen more than we would like to admit. Two sons—one will bring honor and blessing upon his parents while the other will bring grief and dishonor. What makes one child accept discipline and the other reject it?

Whatever the answer, as parents, we have the responsibility to confront each of our children with the truth of God's Word; what they do with it is up to them. Parents have a responsibility to teach them the principles of life as presented in God's Word, and the children have a responsibility to learn these principles.

Despite a parent's best efforts to instill godly principles in his children, still the child must choose the path of wisdom or the path of foolishness. It is ultimately a choice for him to follow his own way or God's way. Which way will he choose?

As a young father, I thought that Proverbs 22:6—"Train up a child in the way he should go, even when he is old he will not depart from it"—was my guarantee that if I trained my children right, they would automatically follow God. However, after raising nine children with the very same principles, I realized that my children still have a sin nature that compels them to disregard the wisdom of God. The old saying, "You can lead a horse to water, but you can't make him drink," surely applies here. My grandmother would always add to that saying, "But you can rub salt in his mouth!" We must always do everything we can to encourage our children's acceptance of God's ways.

But have you ever asked yourself, "Why did Abel choose to follow God and Cain did not? Why did Solomon choose wisdom and Absalom choose foolishness?" When godly principles are modeled and presented to children as they grow up, many will determine that God's way is the path to follow. But what does a parent do if they do not?

In practical terms, while the child is still very young, I believe that corporal punishment can be very effective. A good old-fashioned "spanking" can do a world of good to correct behavior. The Bible says in Proverbs 13:24 that he who withholds his rod "hates his son." Parents who discipline their children demonstrate their love for them. As the child approaches manhood (what the world calls adolescence), however, I believe other more mature tactics should be used.

1 Corinthians 13:11 says, "When I was a child, I used to speak like a child, think like a child, reason like a child; when I became a man, I did away with childish things." When a child becomes a man, it is time to discipline him as such. The discipline must take on much more serious consequences. Privileges that matter a lot to them can be taken away. Limiting his freedom can make him think twice before continuing to behave in a way that results in more freedom lost. After all, in the adult world, infractions of societal law will be dealt with harshly—it is called "prison." Let

your child experience a "trial run" of this in your home by taking away his freedom for a short time ("grounding").

Some children will choose to experience life and make their own mistakes rather than learn from yours or others'. Traveling along that road will produce heartaches, and if they do return, they will be scarred by the consequences of sin. In the story of the prodigal son, the father provides a great example for parents to follow if they face a similar situation. When a prodigal leaves, parents often wonder what their response should be. In Scripture, did the father run after his prodigal son? No, he did not. As much as he loved him, he allowed him to leave and then waited for him to "come to his senses" (Luke 15:17). The father remained on the porch and gave his son to God, knowing that his Heavenly Father loved his son even more than he did. He waited and, I imagine, he prayed.

When a prodigal son or daughter returns, there is an indescribable joy within a praying parent's heart. The father in the biblical account could hardly contain himself. That will always be our response if we have been waiting expectantly.

But what about a child who remains determined to reject the godly principles by which he was raised? A parent, still, must NEVER give up! Or, as the Bible says, "Let us not lose heart in doing good" (Galatians 6:9). Just as God so loved the world, knowing some would reject Him, parents must always continue to love their children and pray for them, even in the face of rejection. There is no grief like a parent's grief for a child who rejects the principles he has been taught. In Genesis 28, we find an example of a son (Esau) who deliberately makes decisions he knows will displease his father (Isaac). This is the trap of a fool. He does foolish things deliberately.

Even when dealing with an adult child who has chosen the path of a fool, a parent must continue to reach out in love and continue to pray. One of the best things a parent can do in this situation is remember to rejoice and encourage those children who have chosen the path of wisdom. We can never be so grieved for a foolish child that we cease to be a guide and inspiration for those wiser children who are still navigating through life. Life is challenging for wise children, too. Be there for them.

The Ongoing Task of Parenthood

Even though all of my children are now grown and out of our home, I still feel the responsibility to give guidance to them when I feel it necessary. I recently wrote the following letter to my children concerning an area that has become increasingly confusing for young Christians today:

An open letter to my children,

As your father, one of my jobs has always been to be your protector. God gave each one of you to your mother and me to love and to give our very best guidance to. Sometimes, that guidance has been easy and gentle, but sometimes, it has had to be hard and not so gentle. In all cases, though, my advice to you has been given for the purpose of helping you navigate through the land mines that Satan has strategically placed in your path that he hopes will cause untold destruction for you and those you love.

In recent weeks, I have been reminded of one of those landmines that I have seen do so much damage in the lives of individuals I have known throughout my life. That landmine is alcohol. As you know, both of my parents died when I was 10 years old. I don't have a lot of memories of them, but the saddest memories I have of them all involved the use of alcohol. I observed at a very early age that alcohol did not enhance our family life, and I knew I did not ever want it to be a part of my life.

Alcohol was abundant in Vietnam, but I saw how it changed the mental condition of the soldiers I was around and knew that, as a Christian, to join in their drinking would not help my witness to the guys who did not know Christ.

As a police officer in Houston, I responded to count-less accident scenes where alcohol had played a major role in the deadly outcomes. I remember one partic-ularly tragic event where I sat in my patrol car with a Christian man who wept in disbelief at the death he had caused by drinking "just one too many." He kept crying out in repentance, begging God to forgive him. I assured him that God could, indeed, forgive him. He never intended to get drunk and claimed he had never been drunk before, but, unfortunately, even as a forgiven man, he could do nothing to bring back the life of the 3-year-old little girl he was now responsi-ble for killing. He and his family would have to live with the consequences of his actions for the rest of their lives.

As a pastor, I have witnessed the devastation that alcohol can bring upon anyone who chooses to play around with it. I have seen marriages torn apart because of the consumption of alcohol. I have seen jobs lost and ministries ruined because of alcohol. I have seen innocent children carry scars caused by their drinking parents. Unfortunately, I have also seen the loss of life where the major contributing factor was alcohol.

One of the comparisons that Proverbs uses when referring to alcohol is that it "bites like a serpent" (23:32). I made a decision early in my life that alcohol is one snake I would never play with, and I have never regretted having that conviction. I realize that the trending thought among many younger Christians today is that because they are "free in Christ" to drink alcohol, it is a wise decision to do so. I am pleading with you as my children to not listen to those voices.

I have always taught you and those under my lead-ership that, as mature Christians, the most important and loving thing you can do for your family is to recognize the responsibility you have to those who are looking up to you. If your freedoms become your goal as a Christian, your life will be centered on yourself and your "rights." If your responsibility to others becomes more important to you than those freedoms, then your life will be centered on others.

As a young father, I had to ask myself two very important questions:

1. Could I guarantee that I would never drink to the point of intoxication? Knowing my fallibility as a human, the answer was "no."

2. Could I guarantee that none of my children and none of those God had placed in my sphere of influence would ever follow in my footsteps, and because of their use of alcohol, embark on a road leading to destruction in their lives? Again, I knew that was utterly impossible for me to guarantee.

I decided that I would never intentionally put you, my children, in jeopardy by exposing you to a life that included a father who drank alcohol, even though I might have had the "freedom in Christ" to do so. The responsibility I had as a parent to protect you from this potentially deadly intruder trumped my freedom to enjoy it every time.

This is my message for you as you navigate this minefield. I pray that you, my children, will be alert to the schemes of Satan, heed the advice of your father, and hopefully avoid any of the tragedies that he has planned for you down the road using this very unpredictable serpent. I love each of you with all my heart.

Your father,
Dean Nichols

Even though your adult children are no longer under your direct influence, it is important, when issues arise, that your children know where you, as their parents, stand. You cannot make them follow the wisdom you share, but at least, when the hard times do come, they will know you loved them enough to tell them the truth.

Conclusion

If you, as a parent, will seek wisdom from the book of Proverbs as you would seek for hidden treasure, you will find comfort and solutions to the various problems you will encounter along the road of parenthood. It is not a job for the faint of heart.

In this modern world, where the definition of manhood is constantly changing, some boys, like Peter Pan, may choose to never grow up; to continue on the path of foolishness, spending their time here on earth in a "Neverland." Our job as parents, however, will always be to direct our sons to the Truth that never changes.

Immerse your sons in the wisdom of Proverbs, but also immerse yourself in that same wisdom so that you can be prepared to respond as the godly parent the Lord has called you to be, no matter what you may encounter along the way. Through our example and through the wisdom of Proverbs, our sons can become lighthouses in their generation and to their sons, who, like all men before them, desperately need to discover what it really means to "be a man."

CHAPTER 5

RAISING GIRLS IN A SEX-SATURATED CULTURE

By Mark and Carmen Howell

One day, we asked our airline pilot friend to describe his job in one sentence. His reply was humorous, enlightening, and somewhat alarming.

"My job," he quipped, "consists of hours and hours of routine boredom punctuated with an occasional moment of sheer terror." Recognizing the hyperbole in his reply, his point came across loud and clear—his job required him to always be prepared for the unexpected.

Much like our friend's description of his flying career, parenting can bring a similar experience. At some point in their journey, every parent ultimately learns that parenting is not for the faint of heart. Hours and hours of routine parenting are often punctuated by times of crisis when the training and resolve of even the most seasoned parents are put to the test.

An airline pilot spends hours of training in a variety of simulated adverse conditions to prepare for those tenuous moments when the "unexpected" occurs. Parenting children is much different, however. Much of our training is "on the job" training where we learn as we go. All too often, when the "unexpected" occurs, we are left scratching our heads, not knowing what course of action we should take to "remedy" the problem.

In a moment of complete honesty, 15th-century English poet John Wilmot once admitted, "Before I got married, I had six theories about raising children. Now I have six children and no theories." Still, despite its many challenges, parenting is a blessing, not a curse. King Solomon spoke of this blessing: "Behold, children are a gift of the Lord, the fruit of the womb is a reward. Like arrows in the hand of a warrior, so are the children of one's youth" (Psalm 127:3-4). Indeed, the calling to be a parent is a blessing like no other.

The Culture is Not Our Children's Friend

Knowing the "blessing" of parenting is one thing; experiencing it is another thing altogether. As the parents of two daughters, we know firsthand the challenges of raising children in 21st-century America. At times, we have even viewed our assignment of raising godly girls as a nearly impossible task.

Today's anti-God, sex-crazed, post-Christian culture is no friend to Christian parenting. As James Dobson notes, the rising "floodwaters" of a godless culture threaten to drown our children. Concerning the powerful influence of culture upon them, he writes:

> We should never underestimate its force, which is like a powerful river that carries everything downstream with it. You can and must help your youngsters avoid being swept into unknown waters. Protecting them from its ravages is far easier when they are young, of course—it becomes increasingly more difficult with the passage of time. That is why a primary goal of parenting should be to introduce your children to moral and spiritual values during the early years. These underpinnings will help keep them afloat when the floodwaters come in the spring.[45]

[45]James Dobson, *Bringing Up Girls* (Carol Stream, IL: Tyndale House, 2010), 151.

We have watched firsthand how the seductive and alluring enticements of culture have influenced our daughter's impressionable minds. Arguably, one of Satan's most effective methods for destroying lives and ruining relationships is sexual sin. We live in a sex-saturated society that often places young girls in its crosshairs. From immodest clothing to sex-saturated television, our daughters are exposed daily to a myriad of alluring enticements. To be sexually active in conduct or seductively appealing in dress is viewed as normal in our world.

It is no accident that pornography is a $50-billion industry. Sex sells, and a lot of people are buying it. We should not be surprised by this. The New Testament is far from silent on the issue of sex. New Testament Christians faced similar challenges regarding their own moral purity. In fact, the parallels between the Greco-Roman culture of the New Testament and our modern culture are striking. From immorality on the streets of Thessalonica to prostitution in the temples of Corinth, if a person was looking for sex in the first century, he could easily find it. Today, from HBO and movie screens to websites and sexting, if you want sex where you live, you can easily find it too. It's here, it's accessible, and it's destroying countless lives.

We have sought to help our girls understand the long-term consequences of sexual sin by reminding them to consider future repercussions before opting for immediate gratification. What our culture will never tell a young, impressionable child is that a fascination with sex comes at a great price. In his insightful book, *Finally Free*, Heath Lambert illustrates the destructive nature of sexual sin, specifically as it relates to pornography. He describes the devastating and downward trajectory of a life ravaged by sexual sin:

> "[It] has now chewed them up and spit them out. At the beginning of the journey, watching people commit acts of sexual immorality seemed fun, intriguing, comforting, and exhilarating. Now, the sin has bitten back hard. Their hearts are weighed down with guilt, their

relationships are strained, their view of sex is corrupted, and their Christian witness is marred."[46]

At some point, sexual sin always comes out of the closet. We thus remind our girls that to flaunt their sexuality in a manner outside of God's design has the potential not only to hurt them, but also to negatively affect the lives of many others.

Sexual sin destroys lives, wrecks marriages, strains relationships, ruins testimonies, and poisons the minds of our children. It is sobering to consider how every new life parents bring into the world could potentially be affected by our sex-saturated society. To combat sexual sin, we must teach our children how to identify the dangers lurking in the world around them. We must also show them where to go for help. Hence, from infancy, we must teach our children to view their world through biblical lenses—to live life with a biblical worldview. This is one of the single most important aspects of parenting. We must teach our children to love, honor, and obey the Scriptures (Deuteronomy 6). When they honor God's Word, they also honor the God who gave them His Word.

God's Greatest Desire for Our Daughters

We recognize that God's greatest desire for our daughters is not for them to obey and honor us (though this is not unimportant). His greatest desire for them is that they make Him their greatest desire. We have thus sought to teach them how every aspect of their lives must hinge upon their relationship with Him. While knowing the facts about God is vital, those facts must produce a desire to acknowledge God for who He is. We desire for our girls to "boast" that they understand and know God and His kindness, justice, and righteousness (Jeremiah 9:23-24). When they know God, they will not only do what He says, but they will also delight in what He says (1 John 5:3). The psalmist wrote, "How blessed

---

[46]Heath Lambert, *Finally Free: Fighting for Purity with the Power of Grace* (Grand Rapids, MI: Zondervan, 2013), 19.

is the man who does not walk in the counsel of the wicked, nor stand in the path of sinners, nor sit in the seat of scoffers! But *his delight is in the law of the Lord*, and in His law he meditates day and night" (Psalm 1:1-2, emphasis added).

When the disciples asked Jesus how they should pray, He responded by pointing them to the object of prayer—God Himself. He taught them to honor His name, to long for His Kingdom, and to seek His will (Matthew 6:9-10). This instruction has helped shape how we raise our girls. It provides a powerful template for how we seek to point our girls to God:

We challenge them to honor God's name. We do not expect for them to honor our family name; we desire for them to honor God's name. He is their Heavenly Father. He has adopted them into His family through Jesus Christ. As His children, they should reflect Him in everything, from how they think to what they say and ultimately in everything they do. They exist to bring honor to God's name. When they honor Him, they will honor us.

We challenge them to seek God's Kingdom. As citizens of His Kingdom, their priorities must be radically different from those of the world. From how they occupy their time to how they spend their money, we challenge them to filter every decision through "Kingdom lenses." Simply put, before they do anything, we want them to ask, "How will this activity advance His Kingdom?"

We challenge them to know and follow God's will. We want our girls to know that our plans for them will always take a back seat to God's plans for them. We teach them that God can be trusted. Since He created them (Psalm 139), He knows what is best for them. Therefore, their decision-making must not revolve around what they feel at the moment; instead, their decisions must be guided by God's eternal Word.

We live in a culture where people reject God without giving Him a second thought. God has called us to be different. He has called us to live differently. He has called us to think differently. He has called us to parent differently.

Those who do not know God pursue what seems best to them at the moment, but those who follow Christ pursue God with eternity in mind. The writer of Hebrews says that Moses made the choice to pursue God. He considered it worthy "to endure ill-treatment with the people of God than to enjoy the passing pleasures of sin, considering the reproach of Christ greater riches than the treasures of Egypt; for he was looking to the reward" (Hebrews 11:25-26). The key to moral victory is not to try harder; it is to love God more than you love anything else.

Lessons from the Battlefield

If knowing the facts of parenting were enough, then successful parenting could easily be reduced to simply knowing the "do's and don'ts" of raising children. Parenting, however, is much more complex than simply following a checklist. To be sure, knowing the facts and principles of successful parenting is important. Yet, employing those facts and principles on the battlefield is much different than learning them in a sterile classroom.

For us, raising our daughters has proven to be "on the job" training on steroids. It's been a trial-and-error, learn-on-the-fly experience. Recognizing that no parents have it all figured out, we would like to share some valuable lessons that we have learned in raising our daughters. In fact, to be honest, these are more than lessons learned; they are lessons we are still learning. Perhaps these lessons will help you in your journey.

Our God or Their God?

After years of teaching our children about God, countless hours of praying for God to soften their hearts, and many sleepless nights worrying about their future, the day will ultimately come when our children must choose to make our God their God. Parenting cannot be reduced to a computer program where if you enter the correct inputs, you are guaranteed to get the desired results. This may sound like a firm grasp of the obvious, yet many parents falsely believe that if they simply do everything "right," then their children will also turn out "right."

For instance, many parents can quote Proverbs 22:6: "Train up a child in the way he should go; even when he is old he will not depart from it." At first blush, this proverb appears to affirm a "correct input = guaranteed result" model of parenting. Yet, such an interpretation fails to capture the nature of proverbial literature and perhaps even misses the point of the proverb altogether.[47] Wherever one may land in his interpretation of this verse, few scholars believe that this verse sets forth a biblical absolute. In other words, there are no "guarantees" when it comes to raising kids.

Indeed, the Bible says much about how to raise children.[48] God does not expect for us to navigate the tumultuous waters of parenting without help. After all, our children were created not by us, but rather by a Heavenly Father who loves them far more than we could ever hope to love them. He knows our limitations, He knows our kids, and He knows what they need. Given the challenges, uncertainties, and complexities of parenting children, we should be grateful to God for giving us a reliable "how to" manual to guide us.

John MacArthur is on target when he writes:

> Christian parents don't need new, shrink-wrapped pro-
> grams; they need to apply and obey consistently the few
> simple principles that are clearly set forth for parents
> in God's Word. ... [These principles], if consistently
> applied, would have a far greater positive impact for

---

[47]See, for example, Ted Hildebrandt, "Proverbs 22:6a: Train up a Child?" *Grace Theological Journal* 9:1 (Spring 1988).
[48]See, for example, Deuteronomy 6:7; Proverbs 29:15; Ephesians 6:4; Colossians 3:21.

the typical struggling parent than hours of discussions about whether babies should be given pacifiers, or what age kids should be before they're permitted to choose their own clothes, or dozens of other issues that consume so much time in the typical parenting program.[49]

Still, we would do well to remember that no amount of training, instruction, or education will override our children's personal responsibility to acknowledge their sin and confess their need for a Savior. In other words, despite our best teaching and instruction, our kids must choose to make a personal, life-transforming decision to follow Jesus Christ; they must make our God their God.

Knowing this truth is one thing; accepting it is another thing altogether. When our girls were small, we were in control of how they dressed, when they went to bed, what they watched on television, what they read, and where they went. It was not always easy and did not always go according to plan, but in a sense, we were in control.

We read the "how to" parenting books and scoured the Scripture for biblical guidance. We "trained" our girls, did our best not "to provoke them to wrath," and taught them to "obey" and respect us. Things were going according to plan until the day they began to think for themselves.

Much like Adam and Eve in the Garden of Eden, the day arrived when our girls began to ask, "Are following God's rules and my parents' instruction really in our best interest?" Tedd Trip is correct when he writes:

> Ultimately, your child must internalize the message of the gospel. Each child in a Christian home will at some point examine the claims of the gospel and determine whether he will embrace its truth. ... The child holds the claims of the gospel at arm's length,

---

[49]John MacArthur, *Successful Christian Parenting* (Nashville, TN: Word, 1998), 12.

turning it in his hand and determining either to embrace it or to cast it away.[50]

Our girls had the information; now they had to choose what to do with it. As parents, we must live with constant tension between training our children as if it all depends on us, and entrusting our children to God as if it all depends on Him. We pray for our children's health, education, future spouses, and careers, but perhaps we would do well to pray for God to enlighten the eyes of their heart so that they may see the amazing truth of the Gospel (Ephesians 1:17-21). For us, the message of the Gospel is powerful, but unless God opens our children's eyes, for them, it will always be foolishness (1 Corinthians 1:18).

Who is My God?

In his insightful book *Counterfeit Gods*, Timothy Keller offers a sobering description of how to identify our personal idols. He writes:

> What is an idol? It is anything more important to you than God, anything that absorbs your heart and imagination more than God, anything you seek to give you what only God can give. A counterfeit god [idol] is anything so central and essential to your life that, should you lose it, your life would feel hardly worth living. An idol has such a controlling position in your heart that you can spend most of your passion and energy, your emotional and financial resources, on it without a second thought. It can be family and children, or career and making money, or achievement and critical acclaim, or saving "face" or social standing. ... When your meaning in life is to fix someone else's life, we may call it "co-dependency" but it is really idolatry.

---

[50]Tedd Tripp, *Shepherding a Child's Heart* (Wapwallopen, PA: Shepherd Press, 2005), xxii.

An idol is whatever you look at and say, in your heart of hearts, "If I have that, then my life has meaning, then I'll know I have value, then I'll feel significant and secure."[51]

Perhaps you are wondering what a quote about idol worship has to do with raising girls (or boys). After all, when you think of "idols," your mind turns invariably to the bad "stuff" that occupies people's thoughts, depletes their bank accounts, and consumes their time. Stuff like golf, making money, shopping, a new car, or an insatiable craving for notoriety and praise. While these things can and do become objects of worship, Keller draws our attention to something less sinister but equally dangerous: finding our meaning and purpose in our children.

Think about it—if your life's meaning and sole purpose for existence are wrapped up in your child's ultimate decision to know, love, and serve the Lord, then what happens when your child chooses another pathway? What if she chooses not to embrace the happy, successful, and moral life that you have endeavored to point her toward?

As a parent, your identity cannot be wrapped up in your child's identity or even your child's choices. It must be wrapped up in Jesus Christ—period. The apostle Paul wrote to the Colossians, "For you have died and your life is hidden with Christ in God. When Christ, who is our life, is revealed, then you also will be revealed with Him in glory" (Colossians 3:3-4). He echoes the same idea in his letter to the Galatians: "I have been crucified with Christ; and it is no longer I who live, but Christ lives in me; and the life which I now live in the flesh I live by faith in the Son of God, who loved me and gave Himself up for me" (Galatians 2:20).

Did you grasp what Paul said? Jesus Christ is *your* life. He lives His life through *you*. Your kids, your job, your spouse, and even

---

[51]Timothy Keller, *Counterfeit Gods: The Empty Promises of Money, Sex, and Power, and the Only Hope that Matters* (New York: Penguin Books, 2009), 17-18.

your church are not your life. This is foundational, yet so many Christians miss it.

Please do not misunderstand—we love our girls passionately. We have cried many tears because of them, we have invested thousands of hours of our time in them, and we have spent thousands of dollars on them. With that kind of "all in" investment, it would be easy for us to make *them* our life. But as parents, it is far more important for us to pursue Jesus more than we pursue our kids.

As strange as this may sound, the only way to fully grasp the joy of parenting is to pursue Jesus and His love, grace, mercy, and peace more than anything in this world. No amount of sacrifice for or devotion to our children will compensate for a life devoid of a personal walk with Him. After all, He is the only One who brings the wisdom and understanding necessary to deal with the hurt and confusion that so often come with being a parent.

Furthermore, the joy in both knowing Him and being known by Him is more profound than any accolades or acknowledgments we will ever receive from our children. Only when we truly grasp just how much God loves and accepts us are we set free from the tyranny of looking for our identity in all the wrong places.

As parents, we have had to learn that our self-worth has nothing to do with our daughters' choices. As John MacArthur notes, parents should not measure their parental success based solely on their children's "spiritual fitness."[52] Sadly, many parents ride the roller coaster of parenting emotions. They see themselves as successful parents when their son or daughter chooses the right path on Monday, only to see themselves as complete failures when their child chooses the wrong path on Tuesday.

God does not view us through the lens of our accomplishments, nor does He see our failures as final. He views us through the eyes of grace. This is profoundly good news for hurting parents. Let these words penetrate your heart: "The Lord's lovingkindnesses indeed never cease, for His compassions never fail. They are new every morning; great is Your faithfulness. The Lord is

---

[52]MacArthur, 19.

my portion,' says my soul, 'therefore I have hope in Him'" (Lamentations 3:22-24).

There is also good news here for our children. We often tell our girls how the Lord loves them more than we could ever hope to love them. And, as much as we hope that they can learn to depend on us, their ultimate dependency, hope, and trust must rest in God alone.

A few years ago, while I (Mark) was visiting Nairobi, Kenya, my Kenyan driver made a wrong turn and we ended up in a traffic jam in a dangerous part of the city. Without warning, our vehicle was surrounded by an angry mob. They began to beat on our car with their fists. With concern written all over his face, my driver told me to lock my door and to keep my head down.

At that moment, as I contemplated all the bad things that could happen, I remember thinking to myself, "This is not the noble way that I thought my life would end." Then, just as quickly as that thought entered my mind, the Lord spoke to me and said, "What were you expecting. ... Am I not enough for you?"

When all the "stuff" of life is stripped away and the only thing left is our relationship with Jesus, the real question is, "Is He enough?" We must learn to live out *our* faith despite what our children do.

The most profound lesson our children can ever learn from us is not something that we say, but rather something that we do. Our children must see that our identity, our parenting, and even our love for them is wrapped up in our passionate love for Jesus. After all, if He is not enough for us, then why on earth would we ever expect our children to believe that He can possibly be enough for them?

The Game Isn't Over Until It's Over

There is a reason why sports teams do not record the final score at halftime—the game is only half over. The Christian life is a journey, not a destination. The road to heaven is far from a straight line. It is a path riddled with many twists and turns, ups and downs, and pits and potholes. If parenting is part of life, then we should expect some bumps along the way.

In this bumpy journey called parenting, we must avoid the temptation to evaluate our role as parents by looking at a snapshot in time. Instead, we must look at the big picture. For parents who have walked or are currently walking through difficult times with their children, this truth can be transforming. Seasons and circumstances change. Prodigals sometimes come home. Lost coins and lost sheep do not always stay lost forever.

As a couple, we often joke how God rarely allows both of us to have a negative outlook about difficult circumstances. Typically, no matter how difficult our circumstances may be, one of us is often able to help the other keep things in perspective. It is a bad day in our house when both of us become disillusioned, depressed, or discouraged. Fortunately, in most circumstances, at least one of us can see the big picture. In other words, it is always comforting to hear someone tell you, "Cheer up. Things are not as bad as you think they are."

Let this truth sink in: The heartbreaks through which we walk with our children are most likely not as catastrophic as we think they are. While a snapshot in time may reveal a stormy season in our journey, a long-term view may reveal the warm rays of sunshine breaking through the clouds.

Think for a moment about a woman named Naomi. Read the first chapter of Ruth and observe how many times she describes her present circumstances as "bitter." Note carefully how she even suggests that the "hand of the Lord" is against her (Ruth 1:13).

Looking at her bleak, dark circumstances, she has every reason to have a pessimistic outlook about her life. She lost a husband, two sons, and even her personal dignity as she was forced to beg for bread. The story of Naomi, however, does not end in the first chapter of Ruth. Remember, God never tallies the final score in the middle of the game. You see, Naomi's life is part of a larger narrative. It is the narrative of the Gospel. In chapter 1, God is far from finished with her; and if we still have chapters remaining in our story, it is entirely possible that He is far from finished with us, either—or our children.

As we have walked through dark days with our daughters, we have never lost heart because we are confident that God does not tally the score until the end of the game. The second half of their lives is still to be played. And the second half of your children's lives are, as well. With God towering over both you and your children, the second half may very well reveal a much different story than the first chapter.

A few years ago, while visiting a small Argentinian town in the foothills of the Andes Mountains, I (Mark) was awestruck by the surrounding beauty of the landscape. From nearly every vantage point in town, I could see the towering peaks off in the distance. Curious, I asked a local shop owner if he ever tired of seeing the majestic mountains in the distance. I will never forget his reply: "I hardly even notice them."

I thought to myself, "How could it be possible for one to be surrounded by the majesty of the Andes Mountains and yet miss their beauty?" When you see the same thing every day, perhaps the glory begins to fade. Whatever you do, please do not allow your familiarity with God to cloud your view of His transforming power. Do not allow your present challenges to obscure His wonderful glory.

Nothing is too difficult for Him. He loves you and He loves your children. "What then shall we say to these things? If God is for us, who can be against us?" (Romans 8:31, ESV).

CHAPTER 6

RAISING TEENAGERS TO LIVE ON MISSION FOR GOD

By Justin and Sarah Buchanan

Charles sat down next to the fire amidst the cluster of grass huts within the clearing of the dense African jungle. He and his traveling companion, Alfred, were escorted to the village by an African man who stepped out of the jungle donned in nothing more than a threadbare shirt while holding a bow and arrows in his left hand and a basket of sweet potatoes and maize in his right. When they arrived in the village, the children ceased their playing and villagers gathered around Charles and his friend. The villagers smiled at the two men, revealing their sharpened teeth that had been carefully filed to a point, demonstrating the telltale sign that the people in this tribe were cannibals.

Charles and Alfred spoke quietly to one another as to whether this might be a trap. But in the following moments, Charles sought to reassure and calm Alfred's fears while the man who led them to the village plucked vegetables from the fire and served the two men meat and the vegetables for lunch.

That Charles was even in the dense African jungle, sitting among a people with whom he could not communicate verbally, eating lunch with cannibals, seeking a way to share the Good News of Jesus Christ, and uncertain as to what would happen next was certainly a very different picture of what he had envisioned his life would be growing up, especially during his teen years.

Charles had been born into an affluent family in England. His father, Edward, was a retired indigo farmer who had made his fortune in India before returning to England to live in luxury on the large estate he purchased. He was fond of all kinds of sports, particularly hunting and horse racing. He even won several stee-plechases and the Grand National with his horses.

Charles and his siblings were expected to always dress in a manner reflecting their family's wealth, and all the children were sent to study at the best schools in England. Charles, along with his two older brothers, developed a great love of sports like their father. At Eton College, the three of them excelled as cricket players. Charles proved to be a phenomenal cricket player, rising to both amateur and professional acclaim. Many believed that this young, wealthy, athletic, and successful young man would enjoy a future of comfort and pleasure. Indeed, he himself thought he would play for the English cricket team and enjoy fame and pleasure whilst living a comfortable life. But that was not to be.

While attending Eton College, Charles and his brothers were asked to meet their father in London. When they arrived, their father escorted them to the Drury Lane Theatre where Dwight (D.L.) Moody and Ira Sankey were holding meetings. They could hardly believe their father would take them to hear a Bible preacher and music evangelist. The family was a churchgoing family, but Charles always found Sunday to be the most boring day of the week. So, when his father said he had experienced a "change of heart"[53] since they had been together the previous summer, it was quite a shock.

Edward told his sons how a friend had taken him and their mother to hear D.L. Moody preach. Though he had been reluctant to go, he not only went, but he went back night after night until he trusted in Jesus Christ as Lord and Savior. Not only had their father committed his life to Jesus, but their mother had done so, as well.

---

[53]Janet and Geoff Benge, *C.T. Studd: No Retreat* (Seattle, WA: YWAM Publishing, 2005), 17.

"There is nothing in the world compared to knowing Jesus Christ," Edward told Charles and his brothers. "Why, since I have taken him into my heart, my whole life has changed. My passion for horse racing is gone, and I barely have time to shoot anymore. You'd hardly know the house either. I have cleared out the large hall and brought in chairs and benches. All sorts of people—merchants, business associates, servants—everyone comes to hear preachers at the house. It is marvelous!"[54]

Charles and his brothers could hardly think of what to say in response to this news their father had dropped on them. They submitted to attend the meeting that night and were never so glad as to get out of there. They returned to school, and Charles was eager to move on and forget about the religious fanaticism his father now exuded.

Yet, when summer arrived and Charles returned home, they could not escape it. Indeed, their father had turned their home into a gathering place for evangelistic meetings and worship. Among those men his father had invited to come speak was Mr. Weatherby. Charles and his brothers had little respect or appreciation for this man, referring to him by the derogatory title of "Old Weatherby." Mr. Weatherby, however, was a faithful witness to the Gospel of Jesus. On a particular day that summer, separate from one another, he engaged the three oldest boys and reasoned with them concerning the message of the Gospel of Jesus Christ. Each of them, including Charles, trusted in the death and resurrection of Jesus Christ that day.

Though Charles lamented later the way he lived those next few years, especially in his making cricket an idol of worship in his life, his decision to follow Jesus Christ and the example of his parents, especially that of his father, led him to be in that African jungle that day. Charles said, "Formerly I had as much love for cricket as any man could have, but when the Lord Jesus came into my heart, I found that I had something infinitely better than cricket. My heart was no longer in the game; I wanted to win souls for the

---

[54]Ibid., 18.

Lord. I knew that cricket would not last, and honour would not last, and nothing in this world would last, but it was worthwhile living for the world to come."[55]

Even in these words, we find the influence of Charles' father, who had told his sons the night he took them to hear Moody, "[Moody] told me that God would give me souls and that as soon as I had won a soul, I wouldn't care about anything else. And you know what, boys? He was right. As soon as I won my first convert, I couldn't care less about racing or making money. Isn't that wonderful?"

Even the way in which Edward lived his final moments would influence Charles. For it was as Edward and his wife were on their way to a mission meeting that Edward abruptly made the driver stop because he had forgotten to invite one of their employees to the meeting. Though his wife insisted they could do so for the next meeting, Edward would not hear of it. He would go back and invite the man, and the two would ride together.

Apparently, Edward ran all the way home and, in the process, ruptured a blood vessel in his leg. Only two years after placing his faith in Jesus, Edward died literally seeking to bring another man to Jesus Christ. The Gospel of Jesus Christ and the example of his parents during those teenage years would have profound impact on his life and work in the years to follow.

In spite of Charles' great athletic success and family wealth, he could not fathom spending his days for fame and pleasure. He even said, "… [H]ow could I spend the best years of my life in working for myself and the honours and pleasures of this world, while thousands and thousands of souls are perishing every day without having heard of Christ?" This became the heartbeat of Charles, who served with China Inland Mission and also worked in India before eventually establishing the Heart of Africa Mission to advance the Gospel into the interior of Africa.

---

[55]Norman Grubb, *C.T. Studd: Athlete and Pioneer* (Atlantic City, NJ: The World-Wide Revival Prayer Movement, 1947), 38.

To this day, Charles is well-known for his story, his example, and his Gospel work. Charles is known more affectionately as C.T. Studd. He practiced in his life the words he proclaimed with his lips, saying, "Some want to live within the sound of church or chapel bell; I want to run a rescue shop within a yard of hell."[56] His parents influenced not only his decision to trust in Jesus Christ for redemption, but to live his life for the mission of God to advance the Gospel and increase the Kingdom of God for the glory of God.

Parenting for the Mission of God

The parents of C.T. Studd had considerable influence upon his coming to faith in Jesus Christ and living his life for the mission of God to see others come to faith in Christ. Parents have a unique position and authority God intends to be used to lead their children in the mission of God; that is, to lead their children to be disciples of Jesus who make disciples of all nations. Our children are not to be merely recipients of the grace and mercy of God but conduits of His grace and mercy by displaying and declaring the Gospel to individuals near and far. God's mission is a rescue mission of seeking to save lost humanity from the perils of their sin and themselves. In the coming of Jesus Christ and the completed work of His death and resurrection, God the Father has undertaken the mission of rescuing lost people that is unlike any other rescue mission the world has ever known.

The primary role God has given to parents is the faith formation of their children. While parents are responsible for other aspects of care for their children, none is so vital as this. Scripture teaches that parents are to diligently teach their children of God's character and commands in every sphere and circumstance of life

---

[56]Dan Graves, "C.T. Studd Gave Huge Inheritance Away," *Christianity. com.* n.p., accessed October 27, 2016, http://www.christianity.com/church/church-history/timeline/1801-1900/c-t-studd-gave-huge-inheritance-away-11630616.html.

(Deuteronomy 6:7). Because of the unique position and authority parents have in the lives of their children, their influence upon the faith and practice of their children cannot be emphasized enough.

In the largest study of the religious beliefs of teenagers in America, researchers concluded, "Contrary to popular misguided cultural stereotypes and frequent parental misconceptions, we believe that the evidence clearly shows that the single most important social influence on the religious and spiritual lives of adolescents is their parents."[57] While other influences upon the spiritual lives of teenagers may exist, none are so strong and important as those of teenagers' parents. For this reason, Michael Widner and Shane Parker write, "The issue is not whether parents will function as an influence, but rather the type of influence they will be."[58]

God calls parents in Scripture to leverage all their parental authority and influence in raising their children to live in the mission of God. While the Great Commission passage of Matthew 28:19-20 is given to all followers of Jesus Christ, parents can and should read this passage in light of their responsibility before God in regard to their children. Parents are to be the primary disciple-makers of their children. They are to teach their children of the nature, work, and demands of God in order to lead their children to live in worship and obedience to God through a relationship with Jesus Christ.

In this passage, Jesus commands us, saying, "Go therefore and make disciples of all nations, baptizing them in the name of the Father and the Son and the Holy Spirit, teaching them to observe all that I have commanded you; and lo, I am with you always, even to the end of the age." Within this is the command of Jesus for parents to make disciples of their own children. The work of leading our children to trust in and live out the Gospel in the

---

[57]Christian Smith and Melinda Denton, *Soul Searching* (New York: Oxford University Press, 2005), 261.
[58]Michael Widner and Shane Parker, *TransforMission: Making Disciples through Short-Term Missions* (Nashville, TN: B&H Publishing Group, 2010), 178.

mission of God for the glory of God begins well before the teenage years of our children. Neither does this work end at the teenage years. So how do we raise teenagers to live on mission for God?

Teach Them the Great Story of God

Raising teenagers to live on mission requires helping them understand the great story of God. This is the admonition of the psalmist when he writes:

> [God] established a testimony in Jacob and appointed a law in Israel, which he commanded our fathers that they should teach them to their children, that the generation to come might know, even the children yet to be born, that they may arise and tell them to their children, that they should put their confidence in God and not forget the works of God, but keep His commandments.... (Psalm 78:5-7)

Oftentimes, we can read the Bible as loosely connected stories, or we can become distracted with plots twists, thus missing the overarching story of Scripture. Teaching our children the grand story of Scripture enables them to see the redemptive mission of God from beginning to end. Furthermore, as we come to know the great story of God revealed in Scripture, we are able to find our place in God's story.

Adrian Rogers wrote that the overarching story of the Bible is God's redemption of humanity.[59] We must convey to our teenage children the redemptive story of God all throughout Scripture and how everything has been to fulfill or preserve this work. To teach them this, we can follow the four simple plot points of Creation, Fall, Redemption, and Restoration:

Creation. God, who is the eternal Creator and King, made all things by Himself and for Himself. Every inch

---

[59]Adrian Rogers, *What Every Christian Ought to Know* (Nashville, TN: Broadman and Holman Publishers, 2005), 17.

of creation was to declare and display the glory of God. God especially made humanity to reflect Him, creating them in His image in order to reflect the image of God in the world. So long as humanity lived in worship and obedience to their God as King, God would be glorified, and humanity would perfectly fulfill their purpose. The first man and woman, Adam and Eve, were to live in worship of and obedience to God and to lead their children to do the same.

Fall. The tragic event recorded in Genesis 3 reveals the deception of humanity to believe that greater things could be achieved in rebellion against God rather than living in worshipful obedience to Him. Humanity grasped at becoming their own god, choosing who or what they would worship and choosing on their own what to label good or bad. In Adam and Eve's act of rebellion against the command of God, they rejected Him as King, ushering into the world a brokenness that left nothing intact of the creation God had called "very good."

Redemption. Yet, even in the earliest moments of a perfect creation ruined, we witness the work of a missionary God who comes to confront humanity in their sin so that they may see their desperate need for redemption, their inability to accomplish redemption on their own, and His promise to provide the redemption they now utterly needed. Into a perfect garden now destroyed by sin, God came. There, He shed the first blood of an animal in order to cover their nakedness and the shame brought by sin. He removed them from the garden and barred their access to the tree of life. This pointed to a greater reality, namely Jesus, who would be that great, promised Redeemer, coming into the world to be put to death by God the Father, shedding His blood for our forgiveness and to cover our sin and shame with the righteousness of Jesus Christ. The greater tree of life would be the cross on which the Son of God would be put to death, but for humanity, the cross is the tree of life from which eternal life flows to all who freely partake of it by faith in Jesus Christ.

Restoration. By His death and resurrection, Jesus gives us life where death reigned; forgiveness where guilt rested; reconciliation where relationship was severed; and restoration where brokenness abounded. God is a missionary God who came into our world on mission to redeem and restore broken humanity into relationship with Himself in order that we could once again live in worship and obedience as His image bearers who reflect His glory in all the earth. In Jesus Christ, God is taking a perfect creation ruined and making a ruined creation perfect again.

Teenagers need to know the great story of God in order to find their place in His story. Like all humanity, teenagers are in desperate need of redemption and a relationship with God through the completed work of Jesus. Salvation is found in no one or nothing else but Jesus Christ alone (Acts 4:12). We must lead our children to know that their greatest need and ultimate purpose are found and met in Jesus Christ alone, whose mission is to redeem hopelessly rebellious people back into relationship with Himself. Teaching teenagers the story of God enables them to see that they are rescued by the mission of God in order to be deployed for the mission of God.

Teach Them to Treasure the Great God of the Story

We teach our children the great story of God for the ultimate purpose that they may treasure the great God of the story above all else. When the psalmist wrote in Psalm 78 of God's purpose and plan for parents to teach their children God's nature, work, and commands, the primary goal was so that our children would "put their confidence in God" (Psalm 78:7).

Teaching our children of the glorious deeds and expressed commands of God provides a treasure map that leads them to the greatest of all treasures. Jesus taught us that the kingdom of heaven is like treasure hidden in a field. The treasure is not gold, silver, money, or material possessions. The treasure is Jesus Himself (Matthew 13:44).

Leading teenagers to live on mission involves teaching them the great story of God so that they may be led to treasure the great God of the story. Our guide in teaching them to treasure Jesus is the book that God has gifted to us that reveals the Son of God to the world, the Bible.

All who hear the grand story of Scripture are called to respond. The response will either be like that of Adam and Eve to pursue our own plans and dreams, living as though we are our own gods, or we must confess the error of our ways and return to God through Jesus Christ to live under His rule. In the former, we treasure what we want above God. In the latter, we treasure Jesus above everything else.

Teenagers today are constantly bombarded with the message that life is all about them. However, when teenagers understand that God created all things, including them, for the purpose of filling the whole earth with His glory and that His redemptive story is about reconciling all things to Himself to restore us unto this purpose, their lives are rescued from the dead-end pursuit of their own pleasure and glory in the treasuring of other things, and they are enabled, rather, to pursue His purpose and His glory by treasuring Jesus more than anything else. When teenagers treasure Jesus more than anything else in this world, they will treasure what He treasures, especially His mission to seek and to save the lost.[60]

Teaching teenagers to treasure Jesus involves more than mere words. We must couple together with our words lives that demonstrate the greatness of Jesus above all things. Our lives must resonate with the message that we give all that we have and all that we are to take hold of Jesus alone. We dare not place before our teenagers anything that competes with Jesus as the premier

---

[60]See Luke 19:10—"For the Son of Man has come to seek and to save that which was lost."

object of our worship and obedience, no matter how good or noble the secondary object may be. The western world has grown really fond of placing sports, hobbies, and personal goals as the object of our true affection. We sacrifice time with God for time pursuing those things. We are consumed in our minds with affection for those things more than a hunger and thirst to grow in the grace, knowledge, and obedience of Jesus Christ.[61]

Treasuring Jesus Christ more than anything else in this world leads to treasuring His mission. While motivators of duty or trusting in a perverted Gospel that inverts trusting in Jesus' completed work for salvation to trusting in our own work to earn salvation can temporarily lead to works of service, the only pure and Gospel-centered motivation to live on mission is to live for the glory of the great treasure we have received in the Gospel, Jesus Christ.

Teenagers will be the Mirror to Your Image

All of this leads us to practically state the obvious: What you display as a parent, your teenagers will reflect in their lives.[62] Just as children inherit their physical traits from parents, so, too, do they often receive their spiritual traits from the teaching that flows from the lips and lives of their parents. If the redemptive story and mission of God do not shape your life, theirs will go untouched. If we speak of Jesus being our greatest treasure and yet our children observe an idol in our lives that receives greater affection, devotion, and worship, they, too, will discard Jesus for a god they find more suitable to their interests, pursuits, and lives. They will conclude that Jesus may be good to talk about at certain times or in certain settings, or that He can be called upon during times of crisis, but that He is not essential to all of life and to be

---

[61]See Matthew 6:21—"For where your treasure is, there your heart will be also."
[62]As already noted elsewhere in this volume, this is not *always* the case. Certainly, teenagers have free will, and so they are free to rebel against parents who try to raise them according to God's Word. On the opposite side of the coin, if they are raised in unbiblical ways by nonbelieving parents, teenagers can still choose to follow God. The emphasis in this section is, therefore, on what is *generally* the case.

obeyed and worshiped. When teenagers receive the message in our example that something or someone is to be treasured above Jesus, what He demands of us all is disobeyed and discarded, not the least of which is the mission of God.

When Paul wrote to the believers in Corinth, he encouraged them, saying, "Be imitators of me, just as I also am of Christ" (1 Corinthians 11:1). Paul would say he was anything but a perfect man, often doing what he did not want to do and failing to do what he ought to do (Romans 7:18-19). Nevertheless, he was ever striving to live worthy of the Gospel that had redeemed his life (Philippians 1:27, 3:12-14), and he invited the Corinthians to follow his lead as he sought to allow Christ to live in and through him.

Teenagers are not looking for perfect parents, because there are none. Even Jesus had imperfect parents as a teenager. What our teenage children need is to see their parents striving, albeit imperfectly, to follow Jesus in every area of their lives. The overwhelming majority of teenagers (89 percent) who see their parents follow Jesus Christ in this manner not only place their faith in Jesus Christ, but they also walk in faith as adults.[63] On the other hand, when our children do not see us living for the mission of God, the likelihood that they will live for the mission of God shrinks significantly.

C.T. Studd's testimony exemplifies the influence of parents who not only teach with their lips but also with their lives. He had lived in a religious family with parents who were lackadaisical to Christianity. Their spiritual lethargy was mirrored in his own apathy by which he loathed the coming of Sunday worship because it was boring and disconnected from the rest of his life. What changed all of that was seeing the faith of his own father lived out in vibrant colors before him.

---

[63]Glenn Stanton and Andrew Hess, "Millennial Faith Participation and Retention," n.p. Focus on the Family, August 2013, accessed October 21, 2016, http://media.focusonthefamily.com/fotf/pdf/about-us/focus-findings/millenial-faith-retention.pdf#_ga=1.132875596.392784255.1440477650.

Charles spoke of the contrast, saying, "Then all at once I had the good fortune to meet a real live play-the-game Christian. It was my own father."[64] Edward Studd, who once had been enamored with the thrill of horse racing, betting, theatre, card parties, and other various forms of entertainment, had traded his earthly treasures for the supreme treasure of Jesus. As Charles recounts it, his father no longer cared about these things, but "[he] only cared about one thing, and that was saving souls."[65] A coachman who drove Edward Studd around once said in response to the charge that his employer had become religious, "Well sir, we don't know much about that, but all I can say is that though there's the same skin, there's a new man inside!"[66]

Children need to see their parents as "real live play-the-game" Christians who do not wear something just one day each week, but seek in the power of the Spirit to live out the life of Christ every day of the week. If our teenagers were to perfectly image what is being modeled before them, would they be living on mission for the glory of God as redeemed children who have taken Jesus as their greatest treasure both now and for eternity? Would they reflect a life lived through the lens of God's great redemptive work and mission?

Practical Steps

Even when parents agree with everything written to this point, feeling overwhelmed at the responsibility and task of accomplishing this can creep in and serve as a roadblock for moving forward. Therefore, the following are some practical steps for teaching your teenagers of the mission of God and raising them to be released for the mission of God.

The first way you can raise teenagers on mission is by leading your family in regular faith talks as part of your daily routine. That

---

[64]Grubb, *C.T. Studd*, 21.
[65]Ibid., 19.
[66]Ibid.

you attend a Bible-teaching, Gospel-centered, missional-living church is important, but not to the exclusion of the faith talks that happen on the way to school, around the dinner table, and at other times of the day. As the Scripture is read and discussed in these times, every member of the family will be reminded continually of God's mission and work. Therefore, when you read the Bible, be certain to connect the Scriptures to the great story of God's redemptive work and how we are to live out what the Bible teaches in relationship to His will and plan. As you do, pray for your teenagers to grow in the knowledge and grace of Jesus Christ through His Word. Ask God to be diligently at work by His Spirit in their lives, convicting them of sin and leading them into truth, obedience, and worship, so that they may follow Him wherever He leads.

Second, lead your teenagers to know of and pray for the vast lostness around the globe. Jesus prayed for individuals who would one day believe in Him (John 17:21). He also taught us to pray to the Lord of the harvest that He would send laborers into the harvest-ready fields (Matthew 9:38). There are billions of people who do not follow Jesus, and many of those have not yet heard the Gospel. Utilizing resources that bring these people groups, some of whom are far away, close to home will allow parents and teenagers to pray for their salvation specifically rather than just generally.

In addition to praying for those who do not have knowledge of God or who have knowledge and yet do not worship and obey Him, pray also for those who have come to possess Jesus as their greatest treasure to be sent to lead others to receive the hope of the Gospel. A common result of praying in this way is that we are confronted with the question of God to Isaiah when He asked, "Whom shall I send, and who will go for us?" (Isaiah 6:8). Parents and teenagers can then ask, "What am I doing to live for the advance of the Gospel to increase the Kingdom of Jesus? How would God desire to use me?"

A third practice parents can implement with their family is to expose them to the heroes of faithful service to God who engaged in living out His mission. In addition to those like C.T. Studd, who traded the treasure of temporary pleasures of material wealth and fame as a cricket player for the work of missions, you can add the likes of Eric Liddell, Rachel Saint, Amy Carmichael, David Livingstone, D.L. Moody, William Booth, William Carey, Adoniram Judson, and scores of others. Reading biographies of individuals like these and discussing them brings to life the concept of living on mission for God. It also highlights the joys and sorrows and the triumphs and tragedies that accompany the task of taking the Gospel around the globe.

A fourth step is simply to begin to live out the mission of God where you are. Looking at the world stage can be a daunting sight. In the words of Bob Pierce, founder of Samaritan's Purse, "Don't fail to do something just because you can't do everything."[67] God has planted you right where you live! God can use you right where you live!

Without changing your routine or the routine of your teenager, begin to look for opportunities to share the Gospel with those you encounter. This could mean a coworker or teammate, the cashier at the store, or the service representative who comes to your home. Then, look in your neighborhood, community, town, or city for those people and groups with whom you can specifically seek to connect for the purpose of sharing the Gospel. Also, you can make note of the needs that exist right where you are, and you can lead your family and your teenagers to specifically begin meeting those needs in the name of Jesus. Are there homeless, jobless, widows, orphans, elderly, refugees, addicts, special needs, or others you can seek in order to display the Gospel by meeting their needs and sharing the hope of Christ?

While you can engage in the mission of God right where you are, consider breaking up your routine as a step you can take to impress upon your teenagers the importance of living missionally. In what short-term mission opportunities can you participate

---

[67]Richard Stearns, *The Hole in Our Gospel* (Nashville, TN: Thomas Nelson, 2009), 152.

together or individually? Ideally, there is greater value in families serving together than in individuals serving separately. Your church is a great place to start the conversation. If it does not already have a family-oriented mission endeavor planned, you can embolden the congregation to adopt this practice in order to encourage parents in their primary role of disciple-making with their children and to build missional-focused families.

A final encouragement for parents seeking to raise teenagers to live on mission for God is to be certain that your communication about life, goals, and the plans for achieving them does not run contrary to leading your teenagers to live for God's glory. Are teenagers supposed to get good grades in school as a way to get into a good college so that they can get a good job and make a good salary in order to live a life pursuing their own pleasure and purpose? Often, this has been the message we have most conveyed to our children as part of the American Dream. Therefore, teenagers do not think of their school as a mission field, or college days as a way to live on mission for God.

Teenagers are rarely encouraged to consider delaying entrance into college for even a period of a year in order to serve in an international mission setting or with a church planter in North America. We create college savings funds that emphasize that we believe college education is important, but we do not create missional-living funds to help our children have the resources to engage in missions. Whenever our conversations of occupations and jobs arise, we often encourage our children to pursue a job that will pay well, as if making money is the most important goal. Instead, we should lead our teenagers to understand their unique giftedness and passions, asking how God may desire to use these for His glory, knowing that the believer's vocation is a place of calling to pursue God's mission. Regardless of their profession, we ought to be training our teenagers to see their vocation as merely the location to live on mission for God—to love Him and love people in order to display and declare the Good News of Jesus Christ.

Parents often measure their success as parents based on the worldly achievements of their children. Do they dress a certain way or act in a certain manner? Are they educated and performing at the level of peers? Will they have a prestigious job and the trappings of a financially successful career? But God measures successful parenting by the degree to which we have properly taught our children who He is, what He commands, and how to worship Jesus and obey His commands as faithful followers.

Conclusion

God entrusts our children to us as His gift (Psalm 127:3). He holds us accountable for how we use our position in their lives to lead them either to embrace or reject the mission of God. Only to the parents who are faithful servants of God in regard to the precious lives of the teenagers He has entrusted to them does God promise a word of commendation and reward (Matthew 25:21).

We can, by prayer and the grace of God, empowered by the Spirit of God, and equipped by the Word of God, raise our children to live on mission for the glory of God. The world and eternity will be impacted because we do!

CHAPTER 7

EVERYDAY EDUCATION:
HELPING PARENTS DECIDE AMONG
PUBLIC, PRIVATE, AND HOME
SCHOOL FOR THEIR CHILDREN

By Charles and Monica Patrick[68]

What milk should parents select for their children—cow, goat, almond, coconut, soy, rice, hemp, raw, whole, low fat (1%), reduced fat (2%), fat-free, lactose-free, rBST-free, organic? What about vaccines—follow the CDC and state vaccination schedule, use an alternative schedule, or avoid vaccines altogether? What about extracurricular activities—limit activities to one per child; enroll them into any and all activities in the hope that they garner that elusive college scholarship; miss church involvement for practices, games, and events?

Parenting is fraught with a multitude of lightening rod questions like these for which society intentionally or unintentionally judges the parents' decision. You have surely witnessed the rolled eyes of judgment; the hushed condescending comments like, "Can you believe what John and Jane are doing with their kids?"; or received

---

[68]In the interest of full disclosure, both authors were educated in public schools and received graduate education in universities and seminaries. Charles has worked in state, private, and Christian higher education for more than 25 years, and Monica has taught in a private Christian school overseas. They home-school their four children.

those Trojan horse emails full of "helpful" web links to articles and blog posts meant to encourage you to make "wiser" choices when it comes to your parenting decisions.

Perhaps one of the most emotionally charged and divisive topics is what mode of education one's child receives, whether it be public, private, or home school. Larry Taylor refers to this as the "sacred cow of Christianity."[69] This chapter provides a brief history of education in America, examines what God's Word says about education, and finally provides a rubric parents may use in selecting a mode of education for their children.

First Things

Select terms and concepts necessarily need addressing at the outset to properly frame this chapter's discussion and to provide a uniform basis for readers. First, the word "education" is a term pregnant with various nuanced definitions based on tradition, presuppositions, and personal experience. The broadest definition for the term "education" is employed herein, unadorned with subjective trappings. Specifically, education is "the process of receiving or giving systematic instruction."[70] Education is more than teaching and acquiring knowledge. It is the process by which one develops knowledge, skills, ability, and character.[71] Hence, education holistically involves basic knowledge, morality, work ethic, life skills, values, and spiritual development.

Second, education is posited to have a single purpose. According to a recent national poll on education, fewer than half of Americans (45 percent) view the main goal of education as preparing students academically, whereas the remainder split between focusing on preparing students for work (25 percent) or preparing them to be

---

[69]Larry Taylor, *Running with the Horses: A Parenting Guide for Raising Children to be Servant-Leaders for Christ* (Bloomington, IN: WestBow Press, 2013), 32.

[70]https://en.oxforddictionaries.com/definition/education

[71]Glen Schultz, *Kingdom Education: God's Plan for Educating Future Generations* (Nashville, TN: LifeWay Press, c2002; Second edition, 2002), 17.

good citizens (26 percent).[72] Although these are quite admirable benefits of education, they are not the main goal of education from a biblical perspective. The main goal of education is to prepare children to know God through His Word and to carry out His will in the world. Martin Luther stated that education is critical "both to understand the Word of Scripture and the nature of the world in which the Word would take root."[73] As such, education is vitally important. Scripture records that Jesus grew "in wisdom and stature, and in favor with God and men" (Luke 2:52). That is, God's son placed Himself in a position where He assimilated skills and knowledge as a man. Education was part of Jesus' incarnate life.

Third, while education is absolutely important, it is not the most important thing in life. This seems countercultural in light of the national ethos of the American Dream. Lawrence Samuel summarizes the American Dream:

> ... upward mobility has served as the heart and soul of the American Dream, the prospect of "betterment" and to "improve one's lot" for oneself and one's children is much of what this country is all about. "Work hard, save a little, send the kids to college so they can do better than you did, and retire happily to a warmer climate" is the script we have all been handed.[74]

Most Americans believe that education is the key to achieving the American Dream.[75] After all, according to article 28 of the

---

[72]"Why School? The 48th Annual PDK Poll of the Public's Attitudes Toward the Public Schools," *Phi Delta Kappan* 98, no. 1 (09, 2016), 7.

[73]Martin Luther, *The Christian in Society, 1*, ed. J. Atkinson, trans. Charles Jacobs (Philadelphia, PA: Fortress Press, 1966), 417.

[74]Lawrence R. Samuel, *The American Dream: A Cultural History* (Syracuse University Press, 2012), 7.

[75]"Americans View Higher Education as Key to American Dream," Public Agenda, last modified May 3, 2000, accessed January 8, 2017, http://www.publicagenda.org/press-releases/index.php?qid=27.

United Nations' *Convention on the Rights of the Child*, K-12 "education should be compulsory and available free to all."[76]

It is true that education generally affords higher-wage jobs. In fact, the Department of Education reports that the annual earnings for 25- to 34-year-olds is $30,000 with high school completion and increases to $52,000 if a bachelor's or higher degree is attained.[77] However, Qoheleth writes, "My son, be warned: the writing of many books is endless, and excessive devotion to books is wearying to the body" (Ecclesiastes 12:12). Every student, regardless of the level of education, can relate to the truth of this statement. The chief point of this verse is not that the acquiring of knowledge through education is of no worth, but that there are more important things, namely "fear[ing] God and keep[ing] His commandments" (verse 13). Philip May writes:

> Education is not the source of man's salvation that many have believed it to be. For education, however thorough and enlightened, cannot prevent man from breaking the law of God and of his own nature. It cannot force its pupils to choose the right course and reject the wrong one at every stage. Man, in spite of his education, can and often does violate his rights and duties if he so wishes, and he will sooner or later have to bear the consequences; for man is a sinner.[78]

Christian parents are urged to be ever mindful of their children's spirituality. Pursuit of education should never trump one's pursuit of God.

---

[76]"The Convention," accessed January 8, 2017, https://www.unicef-irc.org/portfolios/crc.html.

[77]Grace Kena et al., *The Condition of Education 2016. NCES 2016-144* (National Center for Education Statistics, 2016).

[78]Philip R. May, *Which Way to Educate?* (Chicago, IL: Moody Press, 1975; American ed, 1975), 60-61.

Education in America – A Brief History

Public education in America began in colonial times.[79] Before the arrival of the Puritans, America was a vast undiscovered land populated by Native Americans. According to Good, "The [Native Americans] themselves had no schools ... life was the school."[80] Knowles, Muchmore, and Spaulding agree: "Learning from the elders through example was typically the only way in which Native American children were educated, and in such environments, education was viewed as being inseparable from life."[81] As discussed later in this chapter, this view of education as a part of everyday life is a beautiful picture of the biblical mandate described in Deuteronomy 6.

The history of American education has realized major shifts in pedagogy,[82] philosophy, and intent since its humble beginnings in colonial times. Table 1 illustrates the gradual shift from Judeo-Christian ethic toward socialism and new age beliefs in America. Space does not permit an exhaustive presentation of the radical shifts that have taken place. Focusing on two of today's secular and liberal Ivy League universities will suffice to illustrate the depth of the shift. Harvard University was established in 1636 by the State of Massachusetts with the intention of establishing a school to train Christian ministers. Harvard's "Rules and Precepts," adopted in 1646, state:

> Let every Student be plainly instructed, and earnestly pressed to consider well, the maine end of his

---

[79]Harry Gehman Good, *A History of American Education* (New York: Macmillan c1962; 2nd ed, 1962), 566.

[80]Ibid., 4.

[81]J.G. Knowles, James A. Muchmore, and Holly W. Spaulding, "Home Education as an Alternative to Institutionalized Education," *Educational Forum* 58, no. 3 (March 1, 1994), 239.

[82]Pedagogy refers to the method and practice of teaching, especially as an academic subject or theoretical concept (https://en.oxforddictionaries.com/definition/pedagogy).

Table 1: History of Education in America[83]

Era	Colonial Education	Early National Education	State School Education	Remaking of Society	Post-Christian Education	New World Order
Period (Years)	1620–1776 (155)	1789-1870 (80)	1870-1918 (50)	1918-1963 (45)	1963-1993 (30)	1993-present (24+)
Dominant Ethos	Christianzation	Nationalization	Americanization	Democratization	Individualism	Reculturization
What is Real?*	God Christ	God Christ Science	God Science	Science God	Science New Age	New Age Science
What is Truth?*	Bible Reason	Bible = Reason	Reason Bible Individual Desires	Reason Individual Desires Bible	Individual Desires Reason Experience	Experience Individual Desires
What demonstrates a good life?*	Christian Life	Christian Life Good Citizenship	Good Citizenship Christian Life	Good Citizenship Moral Life Self-Actualized Life	Self-Actualization Good Citizenship Morality	Political Correctness Immorality

Items are listed in rank order of perceived priority.

[83]Adapted from Nehemiah Institute, "The History of American Education/Culture"; http://www.nehemiahinstitute.com/pdf/TKS-Chart-3.pdf.; Schultz, *Kingdom Education: God's Plan for Educating Future Generations*, 45; Gerald Stiles, History of American Education, 1995.

life and studies is, to know God and Jesus Christ which is eternal life (John 17:3) and therefore to lay Christ in the bottome, as the only foundation of all sound knowledge and Learning. And seeing the Lord only giveth wisedome, Let every one seriously set himself by prayer in secret to seeke it of him (Prov. 2:3).

Every one shall so exercise himselfe in reading the Scriptures twice a day, that he shall be ready to give such an account of his proficiency therein, both in Theoreticall observations of Language and Logick, and in practical and spiritual truths, as his Tutor shall require, according to his ability; seeing the entrance of the word giveth light, it giveth understanding to the simple (Psalm 119:130).[84]

Similarly, Yale University was established in 1701, and the *Yale Student Guidelines* of 1787 state:

All the scholars are required to live a religious and blameless life according to the rules of God's word, diligently reading the Holy Scriptures, that fountain of Divine light and truth, and constantly attending all the duties of religion.[85]

Clearly, these two universities established during the colonial period originally upheld the authority of God's Word, but the contemporary ethos of these two universities (and most universities in general) lacks the preeminence of God and His Word as truth and now promotes truth based on experiences and individual desires

---

[84]Original spelling and Scriptural references retained. "Shield and 'Veritas' History," accessed January 8, 2017, http://www.hcs.harvard.edu/~gsascf/shield-and-veritas-history/.
[85]"The Founding of Education in America," accessed January 8, 2017, http://teachourhistory.com/early-education.htm.

(Table 1). A detailed examination of Harvard University's motto and emblem proves instructive on this point. The original motto on Harvard University's shield reads in Latin *Veritas Christo et Ecclesiae*, or "Truth for Christ and the Church." Interestingly, the top two books on the original shield are face up while the bottom book is face down,[86] symbolizing the limits of reason and the need for God's revelation.[87] The university's current motto is now merely *Veritas*, or "Truth," and all three books on the shield are face up and open—truth is relative, and God is no longer needed.

The commitment to God and His Word early on in America's history was not limited to the university level, but permeated education all the way down to the elementary level. The *New England Primer* provides an illustrative example of how the basics of reading were integrated with theological truths. Brian Farmer describes the primer as:

> ... the textbook used to teach generations of Americans how to read. The *Primer* taught the alphabet by associating each letter with a biblical character or a scriptural lesson, and then a corresponding doctrinal truth was emphasized with a rhyme. For example, A was for Adam, followed by the rhyme, "In Adam's fall, we sinned all."[88]

God created three institutions this side of eternity—family, church, and government—and early in America's education history, the responsibility of education resided with the family and church (Figure 1). Brian Farmer summarizes the ethos of the period:

---

[86]The original shield can still be observed carved in several buildings on Harvard University's campus.

[87]Harvard Graduate School of Arts and Sciences Christian Community, *Shield and "Veritas" History.*

[88]Brian Farmer, "New Public School Policy," *The New American* 29, no. 16 (2013). Pictures of the alphabet and rhymes can be found at https://en.wikipedia.org/wiki/The_New_England_Primer.

Figure 1: Change of influence of the three institutions created by God and the movement of education from family- to government-control.[89] Eras refer to those defined in Table 1.

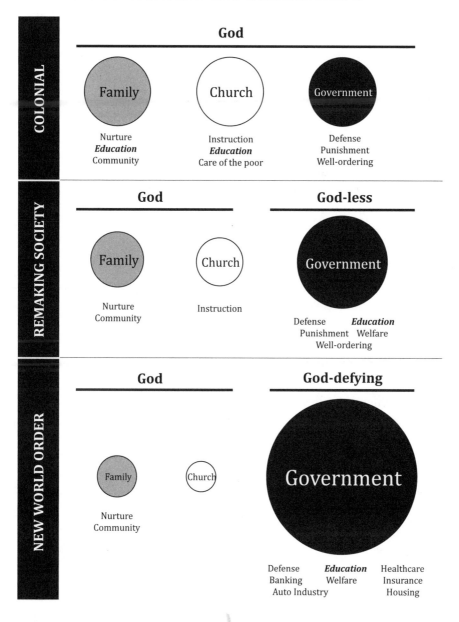

[89]Adapted from Dan Smithwick, *Pillars of the World*, 2013.

"The parents could educate their children the way they wanted to because they homeschooled them or placed them in private (often church-supported) schools of their choosing."[90] At present, however, the responsibility of educating children has largely moved under the auspices of the government (Figure 1). During the shift wherein God was removed, humanism[91] entered to fill the vacuum. A.A. Hodge, then-principal of Princeton Seminary, reflects on the removal of God during the State School Education era (Table 1):

> If every party in the State has the right of excluding from the public schools whatever he does not believe to be true, then he that believes most must give way to him that believes least, and then he that believes least must give way to him that believes absolutely nothing, no matter in how small a minority the atheists and the agnostics may be.
>
> I am as sure as I am of the fact of Christ's reign that a comprehensive and centralized system of national education, separated from religion, as is now commonly proposed, will prove the most appalling enginery for the propagation of anti-Christian and atheistic unbelief and of anti-social nihilistic ethics, social and political, which this sin-rent world has ever seen.[92]

If you have a moment, please reread that quote. It is profound, and Hodge could not have been more correct in his prediction, for almost fifty years following his statement, the first version of the

---

[90]Farmer, 26.

[91]Humanism is a philosophy that emphasizes the value of human beings over anything else, individually and collectively, and affirms man's ability to improve their lives through the use of reason as opposed to submitting to tradition, authority, or God. As such, humanism has no use for the Bible. The main purpose of humanism is human flourishing, or happiness and welfare.

[92]Archibald Alexander Hodge, *Evangelical Theology: A Course of Popular Lectures* (Carlisle, PA: Banner of Truth Trust, 1990).

Humanist Manifesto[93] was written, and the American education system began to assume a humanistic agenda squarely aimed at Christianity. The humanist Charles Potter wrote:

> Education is thus a most powerful ally of humanism, and every American school is a school of humanism. What can a theistic Sunday school's meeting for an hour a week and teaching only a fraction of the children do to stem the tide of the five-day program of humanistic teaching?[94]

Lest you think this statement biased or perhaps too bold, consider what Chester Pierce, professor of education and psychiatry at Harvard University, stated at the 1973 Childhood International Education Seminar:

> Every child in America entering school at the age of 5 is mentally ill because he comes to school with certain allegiances to our founding fathers, toward our elected officials, toward his parents, toward a belief in a supernatural being, and toward the sovereignty of this nation as a separate entity. It's up to you as teachers to make all these sick children well — by creating the international child of the future.[95]

A mere decade later, John Dunphy writes these chilling words:

> I am convinced that the battle for humankind's future must be waged and won in the public school classroom by teachers who correctly perceive their role as the

---

[93]There are three versions of the *Human Manifesto*, written in 1933, 1973, and 2003.

[94]Charles Francis Potter and Clara Cook Potter, *Humanism: A New Religion* (New York: Simon and Schuster, 1930), 132.

[95]Dr. Chester M. Pierce, Psychiatrist, address to the Childhood International Education Seminar, 1973.

proselytizers of a new faith: a religion of humanity that recognizes and respects the spark of what theologians call divinity in every human being. These teachers must embody the same selfless dedication as the most rabid fundamentalist preachers, for they will be ministers of another sort, utilizing a classroom instead of a pulpit to convey humanist values in whatever subject they teach, regardless of the educational level—preschool, daycare, or large state university. The classroom must and will become an arena of conflict between the old and the new—the rotting corpse of Christianity, together with all its adjacent evils and misery, and the new faith of humanism. ... It will undoubtedly be a long, arduous, painful struggle replete with much sorrow and many tears, but humanism will emerge triumphant. It must if the family of humankind is to survive.[96]

The American education system finds itself far from its original Judeo-Christian underpinnings. Now, in 2017, reality is defined by new age ideologies, and science and truth are based on experiences and one's individual desires (Table 1). John Taylor Gallo passionately asserts in the film "IndoctriNation":

Is there an idea more radical in the history of the human race than turning your children over to total strangers whom you know nothing about, and having those strangers work on your child's mind, out of your sight, for a period of twelve years? Could there be a more radical idea than that? Back in Colonial days in America, if you proposed that kind of idea, they'd burn you at the stake, you mad person! It's a mad idea![97]

---

[96]John J. Dunphy, "A Religion for a New Age," *Humanist* 43, no. 1 (Jan, 1983), 22, 26.

[97]John Taylor Gatto in Joaquin Fernandez and Colin Gunn, *IndoctriNation: Public Schools and the Decline of Christianity in America*, ed. Gunn Productions, Vol. Film, 2011.

Luther could not have been more correct when he wrote almost 500 years ago:

> I would advise no one to send his child where the Holy Scriptures are not supreme. Every institution that does not unceasingly pursue the study of God's word becomes corrupt. ... I greatly fear that the universities, unless they teach the Holy Scriptures diligently and impress them on the young students, are wide gates to hell.[98]

If you find this brief glimpse into the history of American education to be shocking, then the intended effect was realized. The point was to demonstrate objectively to parents the educational environment that is present in today's culture. The battle for our children's minds is real. Whether we like it or not, our tax dollars support the current milieu of humanism and hedonism[99] present in America's classrooms. Whichever mode of education is selected to educate their children, parents must be wide-eyed aware of the secular educational environment that confronts public, private, and home school. Our "adversary, the devil, prowls around like a roaring lion, seeking someone to devour" (1 Peter 5:8), and he would be greatly pleased if that someone were our children.

Biblical Philosophy of Education

Is education a matter of personal preference for each parent-child relationship, or are there biblical principles to guide parents? Did educators in the colonial education era actually have a biblical basis for their pedagogy? The specific term "education" is not present in

---

[98]Luther, *The Christian in Society, 1*, 207.

[99]Hedonism is a philosophy that argues that one's pleasure and happiness are the chief or most important intrinsic value and the proper aim of all human life. In the education setting, a student's happiness and high self-esteem are the main purpose. This plays itself out in numerous areas, from test-taking to gender identity.

the Bible. However, the Bible is replete with other concepts that fit the definition of education as "systematic instruction," namely teaching, instructing, training, and discipling. A cursory visual perusal of the Bible or a quick internet or Bible software search effortlessly reveals these terms.

The most critical and quintessential passage regarding education is found in Deuteronomy 6:4-9, known as the first part of the Shema[100] in the Jewish prayer book, so named for the first word, the verb "hear":

> Hear, O Israel! The Lord is our God, the Lord is one! You shall love the Lord your God with all your heart and with all your soul and with all your might. These words, which I am commanding you today, shall be on your heart. You shall teach them diligently to your sons and shall talk of them when you sit in your house and when you walk by the way and when you lie down and when you rise up. You shall bind them as a sign on your hand and they shall be as frontals on your fore-head. You shall write them on the doorposts of your house and on your gates.

Doctrinally, these six verses teach fidelity to God, the responsibility of parents to transfer wisdom to children, and the admonition to bring teaching and training into everyday life. In addition and germane to this chapter, three important truths are revealed with respect to education.

First, God holds parents accountable for the education of their children. This is clearly demonstrated in Proverbs 1:8 and Ephesians 6:4. Larry Taylor, head of Prestonwood Christian Academy, states, "God's plan to train the next generation center[s] on parents. ... We certainly need the church and other training and educational models to assist us in the discipleship of our children, but

---

[100]Recitation of the Shema in the liturgy consists of three passages: Deuteronomy 6:4-9, Deuteronomy 11:13-21, and Numbers 15:37-41.

there is no doubt that God places the whistles around the necks of parents as head coaches of their families."[101] This truth is strongly affirmed in Psalm 78, where parents are commanded to tell their children and "the generation to come" (verse 4) the great stories and lessons of God from the Bible as well as the works He has performed in the parents' lives. Note that parental education not only affects parents' children, but also their grandchildren and great-grandchildren. Parents are not just educating children; they are educating "child-raisers."[102]

Second, the foundation of education is to be God and His Word. Every curriculum, no matter how elementary or advanced, possesses a foundational philosophy that guides pedagogy. Scripture affirms that God and the Bible are to be the foundation of knowledge. The totality of Proverbs 2 reveals the gravitas of having God's Word as the foundation of education—education is not just for this earthly life; it is for the eternal life as well. That is, education is not merely for the benefit of this life (career, financial stability, etc.); it is so one "will walk in the way of good men and keep to the paths of righteousness" (Proverbs 2:20). Parents must be diligent in educating their children, as the stakes are eternal. Judges 2:7-10 is perhaps one of the most sobering passages in Scripture:

> The people served the Lord all the days of Joshua, and all the days of the elders who survived Joshua, who had seen all the great work of the Lord which He had done for Israel. Then Joshua the son of Nun, the servant of the Lord, died at the age of one hundred and ten. And they buried him in the territory of his inheritance in Timnath-heres, in the hill country of Ephraim, north of Mount Gaash. All that generation also were gathered to their fathers; and there arose

---

[101]Taylor, *Running with the Horses: A Parenting Guide for Raising Children to be Servant-Leaders for Christ*, 9.
[102]Ibid., 27.

another generation after them who did not know the
Lord, nor yet the work which He had done for Israel.

Within a single generation, the people of Israel no longer knew
God nor what He had done. This is a grave testimony against the
parents of that lost generation.

The third aspect about education gleaned from Deuteronomy
6:4-9 is a picture of the daily continuity of education. Here, every
aspect of life presents a teachable moment—"when you sit in your
house and when you walk by the way and when you lie down and
when you rise up" (verse 7). Robert Lewis writes, "We often view
spiritual training as an event: God expands it to include a lifestyle."[103] The Shema would argue that the term "school" is a process
rather than a place.[104] School is wherever one receives instruction,
not merely at a desk in a proverbial red-brick schoolhouse. Schultz
posits that education is "a 24-hours-a-day, 7-days-a-week process
that continues from birth till maturity."[105] Yes, Jesus visited the
synagogue and received instruction from religious leaders, but
he also learned knowledge and skills every day from Joseph and
Mary. The point is that parents are not to view education as a
compartmentalized section of a child's 24-hour days.

Contemporary Modes of Education

There are three modes of education available today in the U.S.—
public school, private school, and home school. A public school
is a school supported by public funds through federal, state, and
local sources. The annual costs for public elementary and secondary
schools in America amount to $620 billion.[106] According to the

---

[103]Robert Lewis, *Raising a Modern-Day Knight: A Father's Role in Guiding
His Son to Authentic Manhood* (Carol Stream, IL: Tyndale House Publishers,
1997), 71.

[104]Schultz, *Kingdom Education: God's Plan for Educating Future Generations*,
13

[105]Ibid., 20.

[106]Kena et al., *The Condition of Education 2016. NCES 2016-144*, 134.

National Center for Education Statistics, it costs approximately $13,000 a year to educate a child.[107] There are roughly 92,000 public schools in America teaching some 50 million students in elementary and secondary schools.[108]

In 1991, a new type of public school was created in an attempt to address the woes of underperforming public schools, namely charter schools. Charter schools are a hybrid of public and private school models. Charter schools are publically funded but privately managed. They are publicly funded independent schools established by teachers, parents, or community groups under the terms of a charter with a local or national authority.[109] The charter outlines performance and enrollment goals that must be met. Charter schools are permitted the freedom to be innovative while being held strictly accountable for student achievement. There are approximately 6,500 charter schools in America, representing 6.6 percent of public schools, teaching 2.5 million children.[110]

A private school is a school supported by a private organization or private individuals rather than by the state.[111] These schools are supported by tuition rather than tax payers. The average annual private school tuition is $10,000-$14,000, but tuition varies by region and type of school and can easily exceed $30,000.[112] Private schools are created based on religion, ideology, or some other unifying set of principles or pedagogy that is not perceived to be

---

[107]"Fast Facts - Expenditures," accessed January 8, 2017, https://nces.ed.gov/fastfacts/display.asp?id=66.
[108]Kena et al., *The Condition of Education 2016. NCES 2016-144*, 76, 114.
[109]https://en.oxforddictionaries.com/definition/charter_school
[110]Ibid.
[111]https://en.oxforddictionaries.com/definition/private_school
[112]"Facts and Studies," accessed January 8, 2017; "Statistics about Nonpublic Education in the United States," last modified December 2, 2016, accessed January 8, 2017, https://www2.ed.gov/about/offices/list/oii/nonpublic/statistics.html; "Average Private School Tuition Cost (2016-2017)," accessed January 8, 2017, http://www.privateschoolreview.com/tuition-stats/private-school-cost-by-state; "Paying for K–12 Private School Tuition," MassMutual Financial Group, accessed January 8, 2017, https://www.massmutual.com/individuals/educational-articles/paying-for-k-12-private-school-tuition.

supported by public schools. Private schools include "military schools, schools for gifted children, boarding schools, progressive schools, international schools, art schools, special needs schools, Catholic schools, Waldorf or Montessori schools, and Christian private schools."[113] According to the U.S. Department of Education, there are 33,619 private elementary and secondary schools with 441,500 teachers educating 5.4 million students.[114]

A home school is a school set up at the home. Prior to the instituting of compulsory education in the 1700s, home-schooling was the primary mode of education.[115] In the home-school mode of education, teachers are typically the parents, a co-op of parents, an online curriculum, or a mixture of these. Home school costs $400-$600 per year.[116] Note that these expenses, like private school tuition, are on top of local school taxes that parents must pay. For illustrative purposes, the authors pay $2,100 in city and county school taxes and spend roughly $600 to home-school four children ages 3 to 9.

The home-school mode of education is increasing in America with presently 1.8 million home-school students, representing a 62 percent increase over the past decade.[117] Home-schooling is legal throughout the U.S., but home-school laws vary by state, from no regulation (e.g., Texas) to high regulation (e.g., New York). Parents

---

[113]"Public, Private, Or Home Education ... what are My Options?" last modified March 15, 2013, accessed January 8, 2017, http://www.crosswalk.com/family/homeschool/getting-started/public-private-or-home-education-what-are-my-options.html.

[114]Office of Non-Public Education, *Statistics about Nonpublic Education in the United States*; Kena et al., *The Condition of Education 2016. NCES 2016-144*, 82.

[115]Michael F. Cogan, "Exploring Academic Outcomes of Homeschooled Students," *Journal of College Admission*, no. 208 (01/01, 2010), 19.

[116]"What does it Cost to Homeschool?" accessed January 8, 2017, https://www.hslda.org/earlyyears/Costs.asp.

[117]Jeremy Redford, Danielle Battle and Stacey Bielick, *Homeschooling in the United States: 2012. Statistical Analysis Report. NCES 2016-96* (Washington, D.C.: National Center for Education Statistics, Institute of Education Sciences, U.S. Department of Education, 2016).

are urged to visit the Home School Legal Defense Association to see what home-school laws are applicable in their resident state.[118]

What Mode of Education to Choose

How does one select a mode of education given the apparent historical demise of public education, the biblical mandate of parental authority in education, the various modes of education available, and the situations of life that complicate the decision, such as single parenthood, finances, medical issues, access to technology and resources, etc.? There are numerous opinions and subjective rubrics available adding to the fervor of this lightening rod issue. Here, an attempt at presenting an objective rubric for parents is presented according to the acronym RAVE: Responsibility, Academics, Values, and Environment.[119] RAVE is apropos, as the authors hope parents are extravagantly enthusiastic about their children's education. After all, the education of your child is an incredible opportunity to develop in them an understanding of God and His Word and to implement His will in the world in which they will live and function. How exciting!

RAVE is based on four primary categories that necessarily must be weighed by parents and serves as a rubric by which parents can seek God's will concerning the means by which their children will be educated. Other categories could be added to this list, but they are either perceived as secondary factors or highly subjective factors. The specific goal here is to provide an objective minimal set of categories that all parents have in common. Parents may add additional categories in their final decision if needed.

---

[118]See https://www.hslda.org/laws/default.asp?

[119]In the interest of full disclosure, the authors have chosen to home-school their four children. The rubric provided herein is written in an objective format, leaving the decision outcome to each reader.

Responsibility

As previously discussed, Scripture places the mantle of responsibility for children's education on the parents, and specifically, the father as the leader of the home. This biblical mandate does not permit parents the luxury of abdicating this authority, though it may be implemented differently in the various modes of education. Responsibility, at the very least, means a parent is informed about the curriculum, teachers, administration, and environment and provides oversight of these areas for their children.

Public School. The Department of Education states, "Education is primarily a state and local responsibility in the U.S."[120] Hence, in public school, children are "placed under the jurisdiction of the state government and all legal stipulations related to the state's administration of its public school system."[121] The federal government views education as a government rather than parental responsibility. One Christian Montessori school notes that it should be clear to parents that:

> They are handing their child over to be educated by the government, who has their own agenda and beliefs about education. They are handing their child over to a system that resists parental oversight. ... Thus the public school system actually works against the parental responsibility in various degrees dependent upon school system.[122]

Regardless of the government's perspective on their role in the education of children, parents are still biblically responsible for their children's education. This authority can be implemented by

---

[120]"The Federal Role in Education," last modified July 21, 2016, accessed January 8, 2017, https://www2.ed.gov/about/overview/fed/role.html.

[121]Wuehler, *Public, Private, Or Home Education ... what are My Options?*, 14.

[122]"Homeschool Vs Public School Vs Private School: What's a Parent to do?" last modified September 29, 2015, accessed January 8, 2017, http://oakcity academy.org/2015/09/29/homeschool-vs-public-school-vs-private-school-whats-a-parent-to-do/.

parents being intentionally cognizant of school curriculum and policies, knowing the teachers and administration, and being directly involved with the school and the children's education. A sense of community can be fostered between the parent and other parents, teachers, and administrators as they join together in sharing the task of educating children.

Parents choosing to send their children to public school must be aware of two potential pitfalls. The first is the aforementioned inherent tension in perceived authority between government and parents. Parents must be willing to fight actively for and impose diligently parental authority. Second, parents have to resist just dropping off and picking up children without being involved—a trap that can be easy to fall into with public school—thereby indirectly abdicating their responsibility to educate their children to the authority of the government. Parents have to make a very intentional effort to stay involved with the information and oversight of their children's education and to foster community.

Private School. In the private school mode of education, parents "give its various administrators and teachers governance over most aspects of the child's education and in many cases, the child's moral instruction."[123] Also, private schools are still required to meet certain state government regulations. Hence, a part of the task of education is shared with both a private group of individuals and the government. As with the public school mode of education, a sense of community can be created in this shared environment, if not heightened to new levels by joint ownership through tuition.

Private school parents must be equally wary not to abdicate their biblical authority over their children's education. They must remain informed and actively involved in the oversight of their children's education. This tends to be somewhat easier in private schools, as parents are typically expected to be involved in a myriad of volunteer efforts with the school. In a sense, private schools require both tuition and time as the enrollment fee.

---

[123]Wuehler, *Public, Private, Or Home Education ... what are My Options?*, 14.

Home School. The home-school mode of education inherently provides the most seamless implementation of the biblical mandate of parental authority and responsibility, as there is no layer of private individuals or government sharing in the task. Home-school parents take full responsibility in not only information and oversight, but academic and moral instruction as well. However, whereas all aspects of education in the public and private school modes are spread over multiple people, home-school parents must do everything. This can be understandably burdensome, and parents must remain diligent in educating their children with excellence amidst pressures of life.

Academics

The category of academics in RAVE incorporates all aspects of disseminating basic knowledge to children, including general and supplementary curricula, teachers, and resources. General curriculum includes the academic buzz words of "reading, writing, and arithmetic," "STEM education,"[124] as well as history, philosophy, and geography. Supplementary curriculum refers to curricula that supports the school's philosophy of education or a specialization, such as the arts and languages.

Public School. Standardization is often the academic ethos in public education. Students are exposed to the same curriculum, in similar ways, within a similar framework of time. This method of education affords opportunity for a national school system to disseminate instruction across the country. Hence, if parents frequently move their family due to employment, they can rest assured that, in general, their fourth grader in Montana is receiving similar information and concepts as she would receive in Texas.

Instruction in public schools can be inflexible, with teachers having little freedom to customize lesson plans to each student's learning style.[125] On the other hand, public schools typically have

---

[124]STEM denotes science, technology, engineering, and mathematics.
[125]"Public, Private, or Home? How to make the Ultimate Decision," last modified January 10, 2014, accessed January 8, 2017, http://www.crosswalk.

enough resources to aid students with special needs. Due to the high cost of healthcare and private education, parents who have children with special needs often must avail themselves of the public school mode of education where unique and specialized programs exist.

At present, academically, public school general curricula in the majority of states follows the national education standards known as Common Core. The curriculum's implementation has been extremely controversial. The outcomes of the new curriculum are many years away. Those who oppose Common Core cry out against the curriculum's changes to mathematics and English. For instance, in English, an estimated 60 percent of the classic literature, poetry, and drama previously required has been removed.[126] Literary classics are seemingly replaced with technical manuals and informational texts.[127] Moreover, many of the aspects of Common Core do not align with a biblical worldview. For instance, Planned Parenthood participated in crafting the "National Sexuality Education Standards" of Common Core.[128] While there are potential concerns over Common Core and other public school curriculums, public schools can often possess a wealth of supplementary curricula and resources that can be difficult or costly to duplicate in the other modes of education and can potentially provide great opportunities of learning to students. These include, among other things, language immersion classes, the arts, sports, and science and technology.

Academic performance is an important metric for each of the modes of education. It is apparent that in a population as large as 92,000 public schools in the U.S., there are going to be both great public schools and unsatisfactory public schools. In assessing fourth- through twelfth-grade students, the Department of

---

com/family/homeschool/encouragement/public-private-or-home-how-to-make-the-ultimate-decision.html?p=2.

[126]Alex Newman, "Common Core: A Scheme to Rewrite Education," *The New American* 29, no. 16 (2013), 12.

[127]Ibid., 11.

[128]Ibid., 14.

Education reports that approximately only a third of public school children score at or above solid academic performance in reading and mathematics.[129] Only one quarter of Americans give the public schools in the country an overall grade of A or B.[130] Moreover, 46 percent of Americans believe the educational standards in public school are about right, whereas 43 percent say expectations for students are too low.[131]

Private School. Discussion is henceforth restricted to "Christian private schools" for the reading audience. Private schools are free to select curricula, and supplementary material is often biblically based. As with public schools, private schools can possess resources that are difficult to easily duplicate in the home-school mode of education, such as science laboratories and access to state-of-the-art technology. Many private schools are academically geared toward college preparation, thus the quality of education is generally higher than in public schools. As a natural result, the academic scores of private schools rank higher than those of public schools.[132]

Home School. Similar to private schools, the home-school mode of education is free to use any curricula and is not required to use government-mandated curricula, such as Common Core. There is currently a myriad of curricula available from which to select, including complete turnkey packages to mix-match and build-as-you-go packages. Newman warns that an increasing number of home-education-related companies have started aligning their curricula and learning materials with the national public school program. In fact, at least ten popular home-school curricula produced by various companies now conform to the national scheme.[133]

Not all home-school curriculums are created equal, and parents must be diligent in doing their research when choosing the

---

[129]Kena et al., *The Condition of Education 2016. NCES 2016-144*, xxv.

[130]*Why School? the 48th Annual PDK Poll of the Public's Attitudes Toward the Public Schools*, K8-K9.

[131]Ibid., K12.

[132]Organization for Economic Co-operation and Development, "Private Schools: Who Benefits," *PISA in Focus* 7 (2011), 1-4.

[133]Newman, *Common Core: A Scheme to Rewrite Education*, 16.

curriculum with which they are going to educate their children. To be sure, there are a myriad of education pedagogies available— Charlotte Mason,[134] Classical,[135] Waldorf Method,[136] Montessori Method,[137] to name a few. Moreover, home-school parents have the advantage of customizing instruction to each child's learning style, and they are free to infuse biblical studies throughout all aspects of instruction. Because the teacher is not "teaching to the masses," the individual instruction can require less time at the desk and allow children the freedom to participate in self-directed learning, exploring the outdoors, and being actively involved in the details of everyday family life.

Parents may not feel equipped to educate their children (e.g., curriculum design, recordkeeping, teaching certain subjects, etc.). Parents who do not feel confident in teaching a particular subject have a host of resources available to them for assistance, including online courses for children and training for parents, as well as home-school co-ops where groups of parents possessing different content expertise share in teaching a small group of children. In addition, home-school parents typically are able to find a local group of like-minded parents in their area to seek advice, and a community of resource- and knowledge-sharing occurs.

Home-school education has not always been perceived to be academically on par with public or private schools. For instance, in a 2004 study, Brian Ray states:

> Experience and anecdotes have led many people to believe that homeschool parents were either move-to-the-country anarchist goat herders, or right-wing Bible thumpers, and their children were either math-ematically-limited, due to Mama's fear of math, or

---

[134]See https://simplycharlottemason.com
[135]See https://www.classicalconversations.com
[136]See http://www.waldorfcurriculum.com
[137]See http://amshq.org/Montessori-Education/Introduction-to-Montessori

child prodigies in rocket science who were unthinkably socially hindered.[138]

However, studies demonstrate that home-school education is academically viable. According to a recent report, children educated through the home-school mode of education excel at least 15-30 percentile points above their public school peers.[139] A study where all three modes of education were compared at the high school level demonstrates that home-school students earned higher ACT-Composite scores and grade point averages and transferred more than twice the amount of pre-college credits than students in either public or private schools.[140] Moreover, home-school children settle in quickly at college, as they are already used to studying independently and managing their own schedules.[141]

Values

Values are a critical component of education since they are based on a set of underlying beliefs and they determine one's actions and attitudes. Values that are taught and modeled include ethical and moral values, doctrinal and ideological values, and social values. In this aspect of RAVE, Christian parents should consider the moral and spiritual character development of their children, as well as other values such as work ethic, societal responsibility, and duty to country. Although God's Word is clear that values education is the responsibility of the parent, it is naturally desirable to have

---

[138]Brian D. Ray, *Home Educated and Now Adults: Their Community and Civic Involvement, Views about Homeschooling, and Other Traits* (National Home Education Research Institute, 2004), 20.

[139]"Research Facts on Homeschooling," National Home Education Research Institute, last modified March 23, 2016, accessed January 8, 2017, http://www.nheri.org/research/research-facts-on-homeschooling.html.

[140]Cogan, *Exploring Academic Outcomes of Homeschooled Students*, 23-24.

[141]"Choosing an Education for Your Child: Homeschool vs. Private School," last modified November 18, 2013, accessed January 8, 2017, http://timandolive.com/choosing-an-education-for-your-child-homeschool-vs-private-school/.

modes of education that come alongside parents in supporting their values.

Public School. It is acknowledged that teachers and administrators who model biblical values exist in the public schools. However, as should be clear from the brief historical perspective presented earlier, the values espoused in contemporary public schools are predominantly humanism and hedonism. Even in the best circumstances of a public school in the heart of the Bible belt with Bible-believing teachers and administrators, children remain exposed to government-mandated curricula and textbooks that promote values contrary to Scripture. Children placed in public school are inherently placed in a dualistic environment, one where a biblical worldview is in contrast to a secular worldview.

This is not necessarily insurmountable—Christian children can obviously matriculate through public school without losing or questioning their faith. Taylor writes in agreement that "Parents and churches have proven that they can transmit a worldview to their children in spite of the secular worldview training of the public schools."[142] However, this dualistic environment does require parents to be extremely vigilant in protecting the minds of their children, fostering discussion of secular views with their children, developing robust apologetics with their children, and walking in an authentic relationship with Jesus before their children. Taylor warns:

> There is no arguing that a dualistic training paradigm has potentially devastating results on one's worldview. Dividing life into different parts (secular Monday through Friday at school and Christian on Sunday at church) and navigating through life by operating each part from a different worldview has proven to fragment one's belief system.[143]

---

[142]Taylor, *Running with the Horses: A Parenting Guide for Raising Children to be Servant-Leaders for Christ*, 32.
[143]Ibid., 32-33.

Unfortunately, many parents have not allowed Jesus' sovereignty in their lives or in their homes and do not heed the caution that "indoctrination of social agendas from a young age are causing children to leave their faith."[144] The Southern Baptist Convention reports that a majority (88 percent) of children raised in evangelical homes leave church by the age of 18, never to return.[145] Although the reasons for this heart-wrenching statistic are multifactorial, the dualistic environment of public school and the passivity of parents not teaching a biblical worldview contribute.

Private School. Christian private schools are more apt to espouse biblical values. To be sure, parents pay tuition to private schools in order to define the exact values to which their children are exposed and to ensure there is a high level of discipline and that codes of conduct are strictly enforced. However, parents must remain vigilant and actively involved to ensure the private school hires teachers and administrators who model and promote biblical values, and they must remember that peers may not share their values and can potentially have great influence. Parents remain ultimately responsible to ensure their children's values are centered on the truths found in the Bible. Unless values are strongly present in a school's bylaws, private schools can become lax with values over time as they concentrate energy on academic achievement. Wuehler also cautions that:

> ... although many private schools claim to support a Judeo-Christian worldview, a good amount of them continue to remove mention of the Bible from their science textbooks and endorse the teaching of evolution as "fact," often supplementing that teaching by talking about the Creation "story."[146]

---

[144]Wuehler, *Public, Private, Or Home Education ... what are My Options?*, 14.
[145]"Family Life Council Says It's Time to Bring Family Back to Life," last modified July 12, 2002, accessed January 8, 2017, http://www.sbcannual-meeting.net/sbc02/newsroom/newspage.asp?ID=261.
[146]Wuehler, *Public, Private, Or Home Education ... what are My Options?*, 14.

Home School. Parents who select the home-school mode of education inherently know exactly what values are promoted. They are better able to control the exposure to negative and cultural influences. Because of this very limited set of values exposure, parents must be diligent to teach their children the existence of other value systems and their underlying beliefs so they are not culturally naïve and are prepared in Christian apologetics. An advantage of home-schooling is that there is no dualistic tension between biblical and secular worldviews. Children can be (and should be) educated about secular worldviews without underlying secular values being promoted. For instance, the theory of evolution can be presented as a scientific theory without its humanistic value system devaluing other scientific theories or the Creation account.

Environment

The final category in RAVE important to all parents is the educational environment of their children. This category includes safety, diversity, and social interaction. To be sure, a child's learning space is vitally important for the success of education.

Public School. The public school mode of education can afford the greatest diversity of socialization, as children are exposed to different personality types, ethnicities, and demographics. Children inherently have opportunity to learn to integrate with other genders, cultures, and backgrounds.

At the same time, however, multiple studies show that public schools are mirroring society and becoming increasingly unsafe environments. Wuehler opines:

> The environment of the public school is decidedly unsafe and extremely worldly. Prayer is banned in the classrooms, the Ten Commandments are banned from the halls and walls, and God is banned from the curriculum.[147]

---

[147]Ibid.

A report from the National Center for Education Statistics demonstrates that 65 percent of all public schools reported one or more incidents of violent crime in one year.[148]

Private School. Private schools also provide students an opportunity to learn to integrate with a diverse group of children, though the diversity is diminished due to the economic status required for one to attend a private school. Surprisingly, the student/teacher ratio is not significantly different between public and private schools. The Department of Education reports a 16.1 and 12.2 student/teacher ratio for public and private schools, respectively.[149]

Home School. Home-school education affords the lowest student/teacher ratio, namely one-on-one instruction. Instruction time is also highly flexible, and it is easy to account for sick days and family vacations. Parents can teach at the time of the day that best works with a child's personality and the family's schedule, rather than a fixed school schedule. Safety is also an advantage. Wuehler states:

> Homeschooling overwhelmingly provides a stable, loving, and safe environment in which children feel free to learn and explore without any burden of fear for their own safety. Homeschool parents keep their children safe by keeping them under close supervision and monitoring all friends and outside influences, whether real or electronic.[150]

In a recent Department of Education study, 9 in 10 home-schooled students' parents reported that concern about public schools' environments, which includes factors such as "safety, drugs, or negative peer pressure" at schools, is an important reason for their decision

---

[148] Anlan Zhang, Lauren Musu-Gillette and Barbara A. Oudekerk, *Indicators of School Crime and Safety: 2015. NCES 2016-079. NCJ 249758* (National Center for Education Statistics, 2016).

[149] Kena et al., *The Condition of Education 2016. NCES 2016-144*, xxiv.

[150] Wuehler, *Public, Private, Or Home Education … what are My Options?*, 14.

to home-school.[151] Other commonly reported reasons include, "a desire to provide moral instruction," "a dissatisfaction with academic instruction at other schools," and "a desire to provide religious instruction" (77, 74, and 64 percent, respectively).

In the past, the home-school mode of education suffered a negative blight on its image, namely perceived social isolation. Bridget Sizer writes, "The mainstream perception of homeschool students is that they are an antisocial bunch, toiling away lonely hours at a kitchen table with only their parents for friends."[152] However, with the advent of local home-school groups and enhanced communication via the internet, this is no longer the case. Socialization is not a problem for the vast majority of home-school students, many of whom are involved in group field trips, community sports, home-school co-ops, serving in their communities, and merely doing everyday life with the family out and about in the world.[153] In public and private schools, children largely socialize with their age peers, whereas home-school children socialize across all ages, including intentional, robust time interacting with adults from a myriad of life stages. National Home Education Research Institute president Brian Ray agrees, "Research shows that in terms of self-concept, self-esteem and the ability to get along in groups, home-schoolers do just as well as their public school peers."[154] Likewise, Thomas Smedley conducted a study and reports that home-school children are better socialized and more mature than the children in the public school, stating, "In the public school system, children are socialized horizontally, and temporarily, into

---

[151]Redford, Battle and Bielick, *Homeschooling in the United States: 2012. Statistical Analysis Report. NCES 2016-96*, 11.

[152]"Socialization: Tackling Homeschooling's 'S' Word," accessed January 8, 2017, http://www.pbs.org/parents/education/homeschooling/socialization -tackling-homeschoolings-s-word/.

[153]Lindsey Koehler et al., *Socialization Skills in Home Schooled Children Versus Conventionally Schooled Children* (LaCrosse, WI: University of Wisconsin, 2002); "Socialization: Homeschoolers are in the Real World," Home School Legal Defense Association, last modified March 2007, accessed January 8, 2017, http://www.hslda.org/docs/nche/000000/00000068.asp.

[154]Sizer, *Socialization: Tackling Homeschooling's "S" Word.*

conformity with their immediate peers. Home educators seek to socialize their children vertically, toward responsibility, service, and adulthood, with an eye on eternity.[155]

Final Word

The introduction states that the mode of education parents select for their children is a lightning rod issue. You began this chapter with an opinion on the modes of education, and you are leaving this chapter with a different or same, albeit better informed, opinion. To be sure, the diversity of life circumstances and of the body of Christ guarantees that parents are not going to assess RAVE the same, and they assuredly are not going to agree on the same mode of education for their children. It is also fair to say that in different seasons, there may be different outcomes.

At any rate, no matter what each family feels the Lord is leading them to do, parents are urged to recall that other Christian parents are brothers and sisters in Christ. In matters that do not involve issues of orthodoxy, parents must agree to disagree. Scripture is replete with passages calling for unity among the body of Christ, including Psalm 133:1, John 13:35, Acts 4:32, Romans 12:16, 1 Corinthians 1:10, Ephesians 4:3, and 1 Peter 3:8. In man's sinful nature, it is all too easy to judge one another for decisions made concerning the mode of education selected. Again, Scripture warns against judging others—Matthew 7:1, Ephesians 4:29, and James 4:11-12.

Finally, the decision as to which mode of education to select is a weighty, critical decision. Parents are urged to pray through the decision according to Ephesians 6:18 and Philippians 4:6. The goal is not to select a mode of education that necessarily agrees with family traditions, personal experiences, or even selfish desires. No, the goal is to pray for God to reveal the mode of education He

---

[155]Thomas Smedley, "Socialization of Home Schooled Children: A Communication Approach" (Thesis, Master of Science in Corporate and Professional Communication, Radford University, Radford, VA, 1992).

desires for the children under your care. Schultz shares encouragement from the testimony of Lorin Bourguein that is apropos:

> Choosing a school which your child will attend is often a very difficult task. Every year when registration time approaches, critical questions are asked. Performances are evaluated. Pros and cons are weighed. Each year as you prayerfully contemplate this crucial decision, may I encourage you to seek not what is good for your children, but what is best? Seek not what is important, but what is essential. Seek not glamour, but godliness. Seek not a place that gives your children opportunities to socialize; seek first that which gives your children opportunities for servanthood. Seek not to increase their fun; seek to increase their faith. Seek not tools to make them rich; seek first to give them tools to make them righteous. Parents, seek not what makes your kids happy; seek first what makes your kids holy.[156]

---

[156]Schultz, *Kingdom Education: God's Plan for Educating Future Generations*, 152-153.

CHAPTER 8

SWINGS, SLIDES, AND CURIOUS EYES: RAISING CHILDREN WITH SPECIAL NEEDS

By David-Lafe and Katie Frugé

Swings hang idly. How can the fastest, tallest slides have no one in line? Raucous playgrounds in Texas relax for a few moments when the little Frugé girls stumble into the heart of the jungle gym. Fifteen or more kids fidget with energy but gather curiously together. In their midst is not a tablet or a screen. They are listening attentively to a very young girl with one arm and a metal leg describe how God saved her in her mommy's tummy.

At the story's climax, her little face squishes up and she squints for some reason, "God said, 'Don't you hurt my Eve,' and God saved my head even though He let me lose my arm and leg. But it's okay. I have a metal leg now and nothing can hurt it!"

As her parents, we are always nearby just in case, but little Eve has been telling her "miracle story" since she was 3. We love seeing how kids' fear just melts being able to stare, listen, understand—and also know that Eve's little nub of an arm does not hurt. That is very important to every single kid. "Little arm" is not causing any pain.

This is a fairly common scene for our family these days. As a family with not just one but two special-needs children, we have become accustomed to the curious looks, awkward glances, and seemingly endless questions.

We never hush or resent the questions. In fact, we often find ourselves encouraging parents to let their children come up, talk with us, and ask their questions. As long as questions are left unanswered, our little family remains "other" or "foreign." When we get to talk about our family, explain how "different does not mean less," and show others how much God has done through our girls, we become included, embraced, and understood.

The body of Christ is a mosaic made up of people from all races, cultures, ethnicities, *and different abilities.* Raising children with specials needs, we have come to realize how essential it is to be a part of this beautiful mosaic. Neither we nor the church are complete without the other.

A Difficult Reality

A Mother's Perspective:

The quiet and dark ultrasound room still haunts my memories. I remember my mind racing with questions, trying to listen to the doctor, and the tears that couldn't seem to stop flowing. The doctor could tell we needed a moment. We needed to breathe, to take a moment and try to comprehend the information she had just given us. They took us back to the doctor's private office, and we wept.

After a few minutes, the doctor returned to the room to discuss future steps with us. My heart was so entirely focused on the reality that our daughter's life was in an unknown amount of danger that it took my heart and mind a few minutes to catch up with the conversation at hand.

Our doctor needed to know if our daughter's life was worth potentially risking my own health. Abort the pregnancy to avoid pain. Abort the pregnancy to avoid danger. Abort the pregnancy and make all the hurt go away.

In the blink of an eye, I found myself utterly consumed by God-given motherly instincts, and I knew everyone in the room needed to hear from me clearly one critical statement: Her life was resoundingly valuable and worth every effort I could provide her.

Regardless of any potential risks to myself, I wanted to provide my daughter every opportunity to have a healthy and safe delivery. I'm thankful my doctor respected our wishes and we were able to complete the pregnancy, paying close attention to both mother and baby's health. In a culture that places such emphasis on health and appearance, it was equally humbling and rewarding to be allowed to stand and announce to the world, "All life is valuable, regardless of quality, ability, or length."

Christ's life-giving sacrifice was just as much for our disabled daughters as it was for us. He died to give our children life; we honor His sacrifice by treasuring that life. We treasure all life.

We named our firstborn Eve. *Life.* It is the name Adam gave to the woman after the Fall, after the hope of the *protoevangelium* (Genesis 3:15).

Early on, the doctors gave Eve a 10-percent chance to live. In the womb, Eve lost her entire left arm and right leg. Her right hand lost two fingers, and her left leg is clubbed. Twice weekly for months, our pulses raced as a specialist in Dallas speculated on whether Eve would live or not. We waited for her, and we waited on the Lord.[157]

Eve, thank you for coming into the world and urging those four anxious doctors to leave our room because, despite missing a leg and an arm, you were perfectly healthy.

Lissy was almost the opposite. An early ultrasound looking at Lissy's brain spooked our specialist into a fear that melted away over

---

[157]Psalm 27:14—"Wait for the Lord; be strong and let your heart take courage; yes, wait for the Lord."

the weeks into the perfect birth and the perfect baby. Two days later, as we prepared to leave the hospital, our perfect world fell apart.

Tests confirmed our specialist's worst fears about calcification of Lissy's little brain having been caused months previously by a virus Lissy still carried at birth. She had been born with extensive brain damage, meaning a very unknown and difficult future lay ahead for both her and her family.

Lissy, thank you for being calm in the midst of our entire family's sudden despair. We remember your composure in the midst of our unchecked tears, and your 2-day-old desire to stay with your mommy when they prepped you for isolation. At 3 years old, you may not be able to walk or talk yet, but your ability to laugh and bring joy to all is unmatched. Your infectious laughter and joy is the balm our wounded spirits constantly need.

Parenting kids with special needs is just like parenting normal kids minus the rude staring of strangers, five to ten hours of weekly therapies, added financial stress, constant "winging it" because your mom and aunts' advice pertains to normal baby issues and not your child's specific disability-related issues, weekly stress seeking the best medical pathway for your child's development, and lacking the time needed to spend building a marriage in addition to being a parent. In other words, being a special-needs family is harder. Divorce rates clearly show that. Poverty percentages reflect it as well.

However, we believe that at its core, all parenting has in common these priorities: relationship with God, relationship with spouse, and being part of a solid, Christ-honoring local church. Our experience and biblical understanding is that parents of special-needs kids and churches should be seeking each other.

The Church Needs Special-Needs Families

Parenting two special-needs girls requires dependence on God and on each other. However, we believe that to truly thrive, it requires a good church, too. Yet, too often, struggling parents have to seek out good churches instead of vice versa. Divorce and estrangement haunt special-needs parents more relentlessly than the unending therapy sessions and specialist visits that will not leave our calendars alone.

In our marriage, both of us were uniquely blessed to be raised in homes that were actively involved in a church community. In many ways, church involvement was already a part of our DNA when we first married and then eventually had children. Our upbringing allowed us to recognize the value and benefits of a church community, yet we often see many going without the blessing of such a community because neither parents of special-needs children nor local churches understand the blessings that come from mutual investment.

Like most things in life, the reasons why special-needs families are not more visible in churches are complex and cover a wide spectrum.

Many people have noted that Sunday mornings in America are very segregated by ethnicity and income level. These dividing lines are not crossed by many things *except* perhaps disabilities and special needs, which affect every ethnicity and socio-economic demographic. In many ways, special-needs individuals are a bridge between very different groups. The special-needs individuals who suffer from neglect and low regard are the very people whom God has given the prominent ability to unite diverse Christians in America and abroad.

One particularly unique effect we have noticed our daughters have on others is their innate ability to disarm people, making their hearts soft to hear of God's ability to redeem and restore. Suffering is a universal condition that all humans experience, and when we see suffering in others, we feel acutely aware of our own hurts and needs.

We have observed time and time again genuine Gospel opportunities arise when sharing about our daughters. It is not a forced and memorized speech we give, but merely our story being shared with others. When churches embrace the beautiful work of Christ in the lives of the disabled, the weak, and the "least of these," it demonstrates to the watching world that she is more than empty words on Sunday morning.

Before the watchful eyes of culture, the body of Christ becomes an organic and life-giving entity that spreads through action and affirmation the restoring work of Christ. Churches that neglect to pursue actively and embrace willingly the special-needs community are tragically missing out on Gospel-rich ministry opportunities.

Special-Needs Families Need the Church

Most parents of special-needs children are hurting. If they are going to survive and thrive despite their challenges, they desperately need the community of Christ to surround them, affirm them, support them, and help them.

Parents of special-needs kids do not broadcast all their difficulties, but there are many, and many are constant and reoccurring. Special-needs parents have a lot of bad days and can carry a lot of baggage. That can make special-needs parents difficult to be around if we do not take the time to be grateful and trust the Lord.

Part of trusting the Lord is seeking Christian fellowship. However, our reality is that it takes us two to three times as long to get our special-needs kids ready, and when we do meet for play dates, we are not just exhausted but we usually are carrying some conscious or unconscious baggage from the day before from something as miniscule as watching a 6-year-old boy running as fast as he can, knowing neither of our daughters will be able to do that. That is just sad, but prayer and biblical reflection remind us that Eve will have both legs in heaven, and Lissy's brain will be more than fully functional—not to mention that there are other ways to feel the wind in your hair besides sprinting.

Nevertheless, we carry too much baggage and need help. Please consider listening to us instead of excluding us or walking on eggshells around us. We do not want to be an obstacle keeping our children from the church family they desperately need.

Often, in an attempt to help comfort us, we have heard well-meaning believers tell us, "God chose the perfect parents for kids with such severe special needs." While we certainly understand that the heart behind these comments is never malicious, it deeply hurts. Our problem is that in our culture, when you are chosen for a task, that is code for *alone* for the task. It really does make us feel segregated and abandoned, even though that is the furthest thing from the speaker's thoughts.

We prefer the compliment, "It is such a blessing to see the grace of God in your lives as you respond to God's work in your lives." There is no "chosen" language, no "disability" language. It applies to all Christians who seek to follow God in the midst of whatever trials are in their lives.

Parenting special-needs kids is a daily trial and a long-term trial. No parents would ask for a tragedy like this to happen to their child. While some may suggest otherwise, we do not believe God has an allotment of unborn special-needs souls for whom He is seeking the perfect family. Through our prayer and study of Scripture, we have come to realize that no one understands grieving for His children more than God the Father.

With each pregnancy, when we found out about our daughters' conditions, there were times when words simply could not match the sorrow in our hearts. Yet, we knew we could cry out, "God, your children are hurting," because we believed God knew exactly what we meant. Our Good Father reminded us that He, too, knew how it felt to have sin utterly and completely wreck His sweet child (John 3:16).

Therefore, John 9 is our hero chapter in the Bible. Every word of Scripture is God-breathed, and nothing missing in the Bible needs to be added, and nothing in the Bible needs to be removed (2 Timothy 3:16-17). John 9 had to be in the Bible because it is a declaration that the disabled and their parents are not second-class citizens. It is a reminder that as much as we want to blame ourselves, we cannot. Regarding a man born blind, Jesus mercifully and firmly declares, "It was neither that this man sinned, nor his parents; but it was so that the works of God might be displayed in him" (John 9:3).

In this one chapter of the Bible, Jesus teaches us that disabilities are not the result of individual sins or given as punishment. We believe that Scripture affirms with us that disabilities, sorrow, heartbreak, sickness—all are an undeniable effect of sin in the world. Yet we also believe that John 9 teaches us that God is more powerful than any effect of the Fall.

What sin may have intended for evil, God uses to redeem, restore, and redefine. So, while the blind man—and our daughters—may have been born *affected* by the Fall, God's glory has redeemed and redefined their fallen frames and uses them as glorious instruments that display God's glory and power!

Imagine a church body that passionately pursued special-needs families. Imagine a church that viewed those with disabilities as God's glory on display and gave them the highest position of honor. Instead of parents working in a tirelessly futile attempt to make their children "normal" for a few hours on Sunday, feeling their children embraced and treasured, just as they are. What glorious healing could be accomplished in the hearts of those hurting families carrying such heavy burdens.

Isolated and alone, special-needs families are prime targets for bitterness, jealousy, and contempt. We need the church to help us fight against these feelings. We need to feel God's passionate love for our children through the body of Christ loving on our children. We need others to affirm and treasure the lives that demand so much of our time and efforts. We need the fellowship of fellow believers helping carry our heavy burdens (Galatians 6:2). We need Christian brothers and sisters reminding us of the hope of heaven when our days are dark and hopeless. We need the church.

A Father's Perspective:

In the midst of our first crisis, our long-distance families immediately drove and flew from across the country to be with us. "Immediately" as in, "left everything and came to us." We really encountered shock-and-awe blessings from the body of Christ. Everyone gathered in our small apartment and solemnly spoke Scripture, prayed, and grieved.

Then someone said something along the lines of "Let's go buy baby Eve a nursery!" We had all been praying for almost 12 hours together, and as a couple, we had already been praying for nearly 24 hours. It was exactly the right time to put grieving on hold and choose joy.

We received more than shock-and-awe in-person support. We received a shock-and-awe baby shower shopping spree. In four hours, family and others bought us a complete and new nursery fit for a catalogue cover.

As Eve's father, I felt a mix of building a memorial and building a symbol of trust for God to deliver her. We are glad we received such incredible support at the onset of our crisis instead of months down the road. The immediate opening of the floodgates was so much more than relief of financial stress. It was an undeniable feeling of being loved and knowing that we were not alone.

However, once the nursery was built and family flew back to their careers, we began to drive to Dallas twice a week to see if Eve would live. Those were the hardest drives, and we would sing songs such as "God is in Control." I have often reflected on the need to have a strong church community. I cannot imagine how unbelievers and the unchurched could drive twice a week to find out if their baby will live or die. They cannot sing "Bridge over Troubled Water" for comfort; they need the hope and assurance that comes through true Christian worship and prayer.

We could not have survived those early days of grief without the shock-and-awe ministry the body of Christ poured out on us, and the continued blessings that came just by being connected to a church community. It was, in every way possible, life-giving.

Be Pro-Life, not Pro-Birth or Anti-Death

We cannot talk about being parents of special-needs children without broaching the topic of abortion. Southern Baptists well know that there is a genocide occurring especially against the disabled unborn. Our churches are resoundingly pro-life, and the undeniable, heartbreaking evidence of that is how many of our Christ-dependent and Christ-honoring friends and family members have carried babies to term who were not viable outside the womb. Thank you, and thank you to those who supported them throughout and after.

In regard to how abortion and our culture of anti-death specifically affect the disabled community, some terms may be helpful:

Pro-Birth – The state of caring more about a mother carrying a pregnancy to the point of leaving the hospital with a healthy baby than caring about the baby's quality of life in regard to spiritual, health, and socio-economic matters. This manifests itself primarily as passionate concern and focus on the mother's care up to the point of delivery with little care or concern for the home and quality of life to which the mother and baby will return.

Pro-Life – For the Christian, this signifies determination to do everything possible to secure the baby's long-term physical and spiritual needs, prioritizing the individual unborn baby's spiritual and physical needs over the alignment of an earthly nation's laws with Scripture—without abandoning either goal. This manifests itself in church members being actively involved in the lives of their members and community and caring holistically for the sanctity of all life.

Anti-Death – The fear of death, mortality, and death-reminders, leading to the conscious and unconscious exclusion of the disfigured, mentally disabled, blind, physically disabled, sick, aged, and severely burned. This manifests itself in unconscious attraction to the physically symmetrical and unconscious exclusion of those bearing "death-reminders."

These terms and definitions are our own. They are born out of experience counseling in pregnancy centers, volunteering for political campaigns, and being special-needs parents. The term that affects us the most is "anti-death," or the fear of death. Physical deformities, mental disabilities—these things remind others that "life" often does not go according to plan.

It would be one thing if physical deformities and mental disabilities only occurred among the elderly, but when they happen to the young and should-be healthy, it reminds us of the fragility of our own health and well-being. In a very real and tangible way, our children remind people of death, consciously and unconsciously. If gone unchecked, our unconscious aversion to death-reminders will put us in echo chambers that unconsciously exclude the disabled.

Christians are the best at consciously confronting individuals who carry scars of death-reminders. However, it is the lack of awareness that allows our unconscious actions to speak too loudly.

For example, sitting in a Bible study circle, it is physically easier and more pleasurable to look at someone speaking with a normal face than someone who has lingering facial issues from a stroke. Unconsciously, you pay more attention to the normal face, and your facial expressions and non-verbal communication declare approval that the speaker appropriately receives. However, when the stroke victim shares her thoughts on the Scripture passage, she experiences a different type of attention in which all the unconscious nonverbal signals are negative, accomplishing their purpose of excluding her from the current meeting and likely future meetings.

This unfortunate scenario happens often in social settings to burn victims and the physically disabled, but Christians who are aware of it work hard to eliminate it and take extra care to be accepting, attentive, and engaging. It is awkward at first—even for months—but the heart-felt attempts do not go unnoticed by the disabled and special-needs congregants.

We want families with special needs and disabilities to be actively involved in good local churches. If we are going to be churches that welcome special-needs families, then we must be aware of the ways our unconscious reactions to death-reminders alienate and exclude the disability community.

We would like to say that it is our lack of awareness, not lack of love, that explains the lack of disabled persons in churches. There is a much higher percentage of disabled individuals in the population than the percentage in churches. It should be the opposite. Churches should be full of members of the disabled community, not mainly ministries toward the disabled community.

Disabled individuals and individuals with special needs require a lot more resources than the average church member while they contribute far fewer resources than the average church member. If not for the ongoing work of the Spirit, it would be a lose-lose situation. When we are pro-life, we as churches are seeking that special-needs child and that special-needs family's long-term spiritual and physical well-being. It is not easy, but with dependence on God, it is possible and will resound to His glory.

A Father's Perspective:

I know that kids with severe mental and physical disabilities can far exceed what seems possible or conceivable for most. I also know that disabilities are not an inherently good thing, because they would not exist apart from sin and the Fall. Crucifixion, as well, would not exist apart from sin and the Fall, but God took an execution device and made it something beyond good but inexplicable without sin. I believe Christ our Redeemer can likewise make my daughters' disability-stricken lives "beyond good but inexplicable without sin."[158]

Furthermore, I thank God every night that my girls live in the modern era, which gives Eve a chance to thrive and

---

[158]See Psalm 27:13—"I would have despaired unless I had believed that I would see the goodness of the Lord in the land of the living."

allows Lissy to survive—neither of which would have been possible even 50 years ago. Living in a church culture that actively fights against our anti-death instincts and celebrates their lives with us helps energize us to stand and continue proclaiming the goodness of the Lord!

Conclusion

Therefore, since we have so great a cloud of witnesses surrounding us, let us also lay aside every encumbrance and the sin which so easily entangles us, and let us run with endurance the race that is set before us.
(Hebrews 12:1)

God will continue to glorify Himself. We love being part of praising God and giving people reasons to praise God. Jesus says in John 9:3 of the man born disabled, "[this happened] so that the works of God might be displayed in him."

We do feel the pain of the tragedy that fell upon our babies and our family. But we also know that God redeems what sin tries to destroy.

An example is the Fall in Genesis. After the Fall, the image of God in us was corrupted, but because of Christ's sacrificial death on the cross, we can be believers in Christ. Now God looks at us and sees His own righteousness, because we Christians are covered in Christ's atoning blood (2 Corinthians 5:21). We trust the God who redeems with our daughters.

Chapter 9

Raising Children Beyond the Adoption Day

By Mark Leeds

Into the sun we drove. West. Down State Highway 183. We had left the house with no children and were returning with three, ages 2, 4, and 6—a girl and two boys. A month earlier, they were just a hope—just three children in a nightly news feature on adoption we must have watched thirty times as we prayed to the Father. Were these our kids? After all the heartbreak of our miscarriages, was this the family we had been praying about for so long?

There was no angelic visit, no audible voice from heaven, no vision, no dream. But we were certain. Prayer, the wise counsel of brothers and sisters in Christ, knowing God's love for those who place their faith in the Lord Jesus, His adoption of us into His family—all led us to this moment.

Weekly visits and sleepovers behind us—all to be sure this was a good fit—the rest of our lives before us. Finally, we were parents.

We had skipped man-to-man and gone straight to zone defense: two on three. That is what all of the guys told me. And they were right. Zone was what we needed right then, with the emotion of the moment overwhelming for all of us, especially the children.

Through squinted eyes, I trained my gaze on the road, rush hour traffic all around, shifting lanes weaving back and forth before me. Jennifer was all by herself in the passenger seat to tend to three crying children in the back: 6-year-old Amber squalling, "Bunny ears! My bunny ears! I can't find my bunny ears!"; 4-year-old Jason joining in, his own squinting eyes tearing up in the unblockable sun beating down upon him, "Too bright! I can't see!"; and 2-year-old Jacob adding his wail, his diaper already in need of changing even though we had not even been gone from the foster home for ten minutes.

If we were going to make it through this, we were going to need to trust the Lord. And that is one thing that has not changed over the last nine years.

It is difficult to believe that it has been nine years, but it has been. Little Miss Bunny Ears is working on her driving permit, Sun-In-His-Eyes is taller than Jennifer, and the Diaper Dandy is polishing up his jump shot. Everyone told us it would go fast, and they were right.

Some things have turned out differently than we expected, but one thing that has been exactly as we expected is the bedrock nature of God's Word in making us wise for rearing the children. We already knew it held everything we needed for a successful marriage. The ten years before we adopted the children showed us that, and the last nine have seen us turning time and again to the Bible in our relationships with the children.

So many passages have blessed us with wisdom since that first van ride home. Here are several that have challenged us to become the parents God wants us to be. We pray they will be an encouragement to you, too.

Have Faith

And without faith it is impossible to please Him,
for he who comes to God must believe that He is and
that He is a rewarder of those who seek Him.
(Hebrews 11:6)

Like everything else in life, adopting children has been an opportunity for us to grow in our faith in the Lord Jesus Christ. At the heart of our daily interaction with our children is our faith,

faith that He will give us wisdom in parenting and faith that His Word is perfect for teaching us how to parent and teaching our children everything they need to know to grow in the nurture and admonition of the Lord. After that ride home in the sunset, we found ourselves in a month of transition that turned out to be much harder than we thought it would be. And we thought it would be hard to begin with.

We remember those days fondly now, but at the time, we were just taking it moment by moment. My lunch breaks were extended to give Jennifer some relief from all the morning's activities and to help with getting the youngest two down for naptime. What I had always imagined would be a time of serenity turned out to be the hardest point of each day, often requiring me to dodge airborne action figures and building blocks as one of our children repeatedly refused to take a nap. That same routine would play out again at bedtime each night that first month.

During those times, we would remind ourselves often that we were seeking the Lord in love toward these children and that He would provide everything we need. That same thought would cross our minds each night when it seemed like no sooner had the children finally fallen asleep than we ourselves were falling asleep. Eight o'clock bedtime all the way around. We wondered if we would ever have the energy to do the things we used to do: read, write, just spend time together.

That tornadic first month ran its course, and things got into a rhythm. We praised God for that. He had proven Himself faithful through that transition, and I think, in a lot of ways, that first month set the tone for the rest of our time with the children. Yes, this was new. Yes, we were in need of His strength. But He is able. And He is faithful to provide strength for those who earnestly seek Him.

While those crazy days at the start subsided, other struggles have continued, and we still find ourselves turning to the Lord in faith, expecting Him to give us wisdom in rearing our children. The most common point of need since those first weeks is the need to understand the children and help them with struggles that are not struggles we ourselves experienced growing up. Both Jennifer and I were blessed with Christian families that taught us to follow the Lord from a young age. We do not know the heartache of losing one's first family. But God knows all things. And although we are certain this can happen even if a couple is blessed with their own biological children, we find ourselves regularly helping the children with natural struggles that are foreign to us. We have our own areas of struggle, but they are not the same as those of the children the Lord brought into our lives. Many times, we do not understand. But God understands all things. We take great comfort in knowing that even though we might not know every struggle the children face, we know the One who frees His children from the bondage of sin and death. Taking the children to the Lord with their struggles is not a substitute for knowing those struggles ourselves; it is the best thing we can possibly do for them. The same One who blesses us for seeking Him will bless our children for seeking Him, too.

Speak the Truth

These are the things which you should do: speak the truth to one another; judge with truth and judgment for peace in your gates.
(Zechariah 8:16)

Speaking the truth is another hallmark of our relationship with the children over the last nine years. God expects this to be at the heart of our relationships with all people, but we have found this to be especially important in building a relationship of trust with our children. We knew from the beginning that we needed to be honest about their past. They had had a rough start, and while the oldest remembered it well, the youngest did not, so we had to speak the truth about their past that made sense for the one asking. Sometimes, "Why am I not with my first mommy and daddy?" could be answered with a simple, "It wasn't a safe place for you to be."

As they grew, details were added, giving us opportunity to talk about how it is not safe to take "medicines" you are not supposed to, then eventually the opportunity to talk about drugs and alcohol and what God's Word says about the dangers of sins in those areas. In recent years, even more truth has been discussed as we have sat down with some of the old adoption files with all the details about their first parents and talked about what happened—always in love, always in truth.

While truth delivered from us to the children was one way we kept the focus on God's standard for truth, another was in expecting the children to be truthful with us. I think those three words—"speak the truth"—may have been spoken more than any others in our interactions with the children those first few years. So often was this quoted that, within a few months, the children could easily answer when we would ask them, "What does God expect of you, 'Speak the...'?" "Truth" is how they would answer, but truth is not always what was spoken.

We are certain all families face this issue, but it seemed to be a regular issue for us along the way. Perhaps it was out of a desire not to disappoint their new mommy and daddy, or perhaps it was a desire to find ways to ensure they would have what they thought they needed to be happy, but either way, it was a sin we had to confront regularly. We would talk about the Lord and how He always told the truth; how God is completely trustworthy; how all of His Word is true. We would like to be able to say this is a resolved issue, but still, we find ourselves reminding the children of this verse from time to time.

Truth has also been important to us in our interactions with church members and friends and family. Sometimes, you can get so close to the situation that you do not see the truth clearly. And that goes both ways, both the good and the bad.

On the negative side, we have tried always to listen to the behavior reports from Sunday School teachers and nursery workers. What is really going on when they are out of eyesight and earshot? We want to know. Sometimes, you will get that smile from that wonderful Sunday School teacher who would never say an unkind thing about anyone, and all we would get is a "Well, he did okay today." Instant sidebar in the hall … "Okay, what happened? We need to know."

That accountability has meant a lot to our relationship with the children from the start. We care enough to want to know the truth, even if it means we find out one of them chunked a building block over the Dutch door in the nursery and pegged the preschool director on the noggin. That is the kind of thing we need to know, and the children knew that if we found out, there would be consequences.

But those are not the times we relish, of course. The times we look forward to are those times where we are exhausted and frustrated and it seems like nothing is changing, and then another Sunday School teacher comes up and lets us know how he has seen so much peace or love or kindness from one of the children, and you just cannot help but pull that child aside on the way out from church and tell him/her what a great report you received that day.

Share the Gospel

…Choose for yourselves today whom you will serve: whether the gods which your fathers served which were beyond the River, or the gods of the Amorites in whose land you are living; but as for me and my house, we will serve the Lord.
(Joshua 24:15b)

From the very start with the children, we declared to them the Gospel of the Lord Jesus Christ. Through family devotions, church conversations, and home-school curriculum, we cherished the Gospel and placed before them the greatest of all decisions each one of them would have to make. We always understood that no matter how much we loved them or provided for them or taught them, we would never love, provide, or teach them better than when we shared with them the Gospel.

We knew that the only hope for them was salvation; that the only solution to their hurts and history was the change the Lord would work in their hearts if only they would repent and believe in the Lord's sacrifice, burial, and resurrection. This has been and will continue to be our greatest burden for our children until they all believe in Him.

When laying this decision before them, we have tried consistently to remind them that it is not a choice that can be made for someone else, but a choice that must come from that child's own heart before the Lord. This can be a treacherous road to navigate. On the one hand, we did not want the children falsely professing faith just to "make us happy," but on the other hand, we did not want to hide the fact that it would make us so happy for them to believe. Ultimately, we took direction from the principle expressed by Joshua so long ago: place the choice before the people and set the example for them in your own life.

Two of our children have believed in the Lord, and one has not. This continues to be the greatest burden on our hearts each day; it is at the center of our prayers, and a new hope rises with each morning that this will be the day of salvation for the one who remains apart from Christ. Even though the one has not believed, we continue to instruct that child in the ways of the Lord. This is difficult. But this is necessary.

Sometimes, that child has asked whether daily Bible reading can be skipped since that child does not believe. Our answer has been "no." I suspect this has cut short other requests of a like nature—"Can I stay home from church? I don't believe." "Can I skip the family mission trip? I don't believe." Our conviction has been and will continue to be that my own response to Joshua's question as the spiritual leader of my family has to be, "As for me and my house, we will serve the Lord."

As a family, we read God's Word. As a family, we attend church. As a family, we serve the Lord. But still, I know I cannot expect to see the same things from that child as I will see from the others. Mission trip melt-downs are going to happen, prayers will be shallow, enthusiasm low. We do not discipline for those things; they are to be expected ... for now. But we trust the ministry of the Spirit in that child's heart. We trust God's Word not to return void. We trust the Lord.

Lovingly Discipline

He who withholds his rod hates his son, but he
who loves him disciplines him diligently.
(Proverbs 13:24)

When the children first came to live with us, they were in adoptive placement, which meant they were not yet legally our children, which meant we could not spank them. But we could discipline through other means like "time out." And we did. Often. Because we loved them.

There are a couple of spots on the floor in the hallway where I think, if you lean down and inspect the carpet, you will find two impressions where the children sat, often two at a time, for a few minutes at a time for one thing or another—defiance, fighting, biting. It felt like we were pushing against the tide at first, but we knew this verse well, and we believed it to be true. If we really loved these children, we would discipline them consistently.

Reflections of those same lunch-time visits mentioned above come to mind. Finding two or sometimes all three there in the hall and my heart sinking at the thought of another rough morning for Jennifer, I'd ask, "What happened?" knowing I needed to know but hoping for a day when I would come home and discover that no one had gotten in trouble that morning. Those days did not come often at first, but they did over time. In fact, some of my happiest memories from that time are when I would find all three in the hall and ask the question only to hear them all shout, "Nothing! We've all been good! Fooled you, Daddy!" Praise the Lord for those days!

Although we could not spank at first, we did once the children were legally adopted. I never relished it, and neither did Jennifer.

But we knew we could take God at His word. Always, we would remind them that we were disciplining them because we loved them. I am not sure they believed us at first, but that trust came over time, and thankfully, we are past the spanking phase now.

This was one of those areas where neither Jennifer nor I understood the children. We had both been spanked exactly once by our parents growing up. We had deserved it, and that rod had done its work instantly; we never wanted to experience discipline from the hands of our parents ever again. With our kids, it was different, and that was hard to understand at first, but not once we reflected on the discipline of the Lord in our lives. While we had complied with our earthly fathers for fear of discipline, we both took a circuitous path in our teen years that led to some tough lessons from the hand of our Heavenly Father. Our own recalcitrance in those years combined with the loving (although sometimes painful) correction from the Father reminded us that the same diligence He showed in loving us in those times of disobedience needed to be our diligence in disciplining our children.

Have Fellowship with the Body of Christ

And if one member suffers, all the members suffer with it;
if one member is honored, all the members rejoice with it.
(1 Corinthians 12:26)

Another key to our parenting with the children has been the local church. When we started praying about the possibility of adopting, our Sunday School class prayed with us. When we went on those first visits, they prayed for us. When we brought the children into our home, they gave generously. When we struggled, they struggled with us. When we laughed, they laughed. When we cried, they cried, just the way the Lord designed the body of Christ to work.

Along the way, we have found some of our closest friends while serving in different ministries of the church. I have always wanted to be close to the children in the children's ministry and have spent the last seven years as a Wednesday-night discipleship group leader. That gave me the chance to be close to the children and see how they were progressing, but it also put me alongside mentors who were years ahead of us in the rearing of their own children. Even more valuable than seeing what our kids were doing were those conversations before and after church with those who had gone before us. How had they handled it when they found fifty peppermint wrappers in their 6-year-old's night stand? Other parents have had that happen, right?

But working directly with the kids is not the only way to partner with the church. Jennifer has participated in and now leads a discipleship group for moms to encourage each other in biblical child-rearing. We have gone from inexperienced, naively idealistic parents to battle-tested-wisdom-on-the-rise parents over the last nine years, and it is such a joy to help those with younger children now.

Our local church has been such a blessing to us not only through the membership, but also through the leadership. We especially found ourselves coming to deeper insights into the role of children in the church through our service under the children's ministers the last nine years. Those ministers have helped us to see in practice what we always would have affirmed in theory—that saved children are indwelled by the Holy Spirit and can do amazing things in the Lord from a young age.

This is one area where we were limited by our own experiences as children growing up. Both Jennifer and I experienced children's ministry in our home churches as a "sit and listen" experience. There is certainly a place for that, but there is also so much room to challenge the children who are believers.

I will never forget doubting our children's minister when he told us that he was going to dedicate an entire Wednesday evening to prayer. How would I possibly be able to handle my four third-graders for an hour and a half of prayer when all we had ever done before was five minutes in class? Still, I decided to give it a go, "submit yourselves one to another" echoing in my mind along with those doubts about the practicality of it all. I figured, "What's the worst that could happen?" Not the best attitude for sure, but God set me straight. Those boys traveled with me from room to room set up for them by the minister, and we prayed for lost friends and lost countries and confessed sin and praised God for that hour and a half. I would have missed out on that and so much more if we had not connected with the local church.

Diligently Teach the Ways of the Lord

Hear, O Israel! The Lord is our God, the Lord is one! You shall love the Lord your God with all your heart and with all your soul and with all your might. These words, which I am commanding you today, shall be on your heart. You shall teach them diligently to your sons and shall talk of them when you sit in your house and when you walk by the way and when you lie down and when you rise up.
(Deuteronomy 6:4-7)

The first year and a half the children were with us, the oldest was in kindergarten/first grade in public school, and the boys were home with Jennifer or at the church for pre-K. It was the best way we knew to make the transition from no children to three, and we still think it was the way to handle that phase, but we found by the end of that time that a change was needed.

Three major factors contributed to our decision to begin home-schooling. First, we knew that God had placed an expectation on the family to be the primary place of learning about the things of the Lord. What we found was that even though the children were young when they came to live with us, those early years are so crucial to a child's spiritual learning that we were behind the curve. We simply needed more time with them to teach them about the Lord.

Second, the public school culture was reinforcing behavior that was undesirable. It was not that the teachers were bad (in fact, both of them are members of our church) or that things were completely out of control, but we were getting reports that little rebellious things were happening in school that we needed to address with more time at home. We will never forget getting that report that one of our children had teamed up with another kindergartner and the two had become affectionately known (or maybe not) by their teacher as little "partners in crime." The teacher had developed a system of behavior tracking that involved a clothespin with the child's name on it, and that clothespin would move from green to yellow to red if behavior deteriorated throughout the day. One day, that child came home, and we learned that her clothespin was not on green or yellow or even red. It was on the floor! Something had to change.

Third, we found that it was difficult to develop a deep relationship with our oldest when we sent her off to school each day and the boys were at home with Jennifer. There was some jealousy that developed, but I do not think it was the bad kind of jealousy. Our oldest wanted to have quality time with us, and we wanted it with her, and that just was not possible going the public school route.

This year, the children are in sixth, seventh, and ninth grades, and we are still home-schooling them. We value the time with the children so much in home school that we will not trade it in now. Not that it is perfect. Many times, I come home at lunch and drop in as the "principal." No greater fear has been struck in the eyes of the children than to know they have reached the limit with Mom, and when I get home, "daddy school" will be in session.

Of course, I prefer to offer after-hours help that is not disciplinary in nature, and that happens, too, but when discipline is needed, I am good for it. But more than all those things, the greatest thing about home-schooling for our children has been the opportunity for us to do exactly what Deuteronomy 6:4-7 requires—the constant contact with the children enables us to talk about the Lord all throughout the day. Everything we do can be presented to the children through the lens of God's Word. God's sovereign hand in history? Check. God's design in creation?

Check. Moral relativity of the Pokémon Black and White theme song in need of correction? Double check.

Trust in the Lord

Trust in the Lord with all your heart and
do not lean on your own understanding.
(Proverbs 3:5)

We are so thankful that the Lord has brought these three children into our family. We have absolutely no doubt that they are exactly the children the Lord wanted us to have, and we have grown so much as believers over the last nine years because of their presence in our lives. Being parents has forced us to think more biblically about the family.

Our prayers are for you if you are reading this and are praying about adopting. It will require you to depend on the Lord; force tough conversations about the truth; make you a better evangelist; and teach you the Lord's love in discipline, a deeper appreciation for the church, and how to instruct children in the ways of the Lord each and every day. And we can testify that the Lord is faithful through it all.

Be obedient to what He is calling you to do. He is trustworthy.

Chapter 10

What to Do When your Child Struggles with Homosexuality

By Johnny Derouen

Having served in youth ministry for 42 years, some of the most difficult situations I faced were when parents came to me for help after discovering that their child was struggling with homosexuality. It was extremely heart-wrenching for both parent and child. What should parents do? How do parents respond to their child? Where do they turn for help?

The following are real parent thoughts on facing this struggle:

> "I found out my daughter was gay a year and a half ago. I have been on an emotional roller coaster ever since. She still lives at home and I found out that she had been in three 'relationships' in the past. She believes she was born this way and that only the 'red letter' parts of the Bible are what you have to believe. I have tried to talk to her many times and she just shuts down. She continues to go to church. But every time she leaves the house, I just feel sick wondering what she's doing. We used to be very close but mostly our relationship is strained now. I feel cheated and like all my dreams for her have been shattered. I have no one who understands."

"I am dealing with the acceptance that my son is gay. My heart has gone to the bottoms of hell, it seems. I was brought up to believe that being homosexual is wrong, and I am struggling with his sexuality. I have been depressed for a year since I found out. I just feel so much despair, and I do not think I can deal with this. I do not want to lose my son. If someone can help me with words, please do."

The above words of precious parents can break the hearts of those who love teenagers and their families. As one's faith is challenged, what are the answers and the helps? There are clear biblical helps and solutions, but neither will be easy. People who face this issue are entering an emotional roller coaster that will greatly challenge the faith of both parent and child.

Parents will need to hold on to the biblical position on same-sex relationships in the face of what may be strong, deeply emotional pleas from their child to affirm his lifestyle. This is a painful and difficult place for parents today. It is not altogether wrong for parents to want to see their son or daughter prospering or being happy, yet the one thing that will remain painful and grievous is their unwillingness to affirm a lifestyle direction that is contrary to God's design in Scripture.

Gay teens are usually left to deal with same-sex attraction alone since many parents are afraid to say or do the wrong thing and thus "lose" their child. As gay teens begin to turn to their friends for help and support, most are left with their deepest questions unanswered and find themselves falling deeper and deeper into the gay lifestyle.

So where do parents start when faced with this increasingly common situation? What should their response be? Understand that churches and homes must be places where people, especially those struggling with gender confusion, encounter Jesus, both physically and spiritually. This will involve truth, compassion, safety, and authentic love. The foundations are Jesus and Scripture.

Key Truths and Concepts

1. Walk very close to Jesus

You will need to have God's wisdom and grace when dealing with your child, who is deeply loved by both you and Jesus. As stated in Proverbs 1:7, the beginning of wisdom and knowledge is the fear and respect of God, so start with a close walk with Jesus.

2. Know that God is graciously sovereign and that He put your children in your sphere of influence

God wants to use you! Psalm 103:19 states, "The Lord has established His throne in the heavens, and His sovereignty rules over all." He really is in charge—seek Him for wisdom and grace.

3. Know God's Word on the issue

This is where you need to start. There are seven foundational passages dealing directly with the subject of homosexuality. Stress that the Bible does not condemn homosexual inclinations or temptations, but Scripture does clearly speak against homosexual activity and behavior.

You must be honest enough to desire to know what God, through the Bible, says and to allow yourself and others to work through the inevitable emotions in order to see the truth of God's Word. Passages in the Bible that parents need to read and study further on God's thoughts on this issue include:

- **Genesis 2:18-24**

Then the Lord God said, "It is not good for the man to be alone; I will make him a helper suitable for him."

Out of the ground the Lord God formed every beast of the field and every bird of the sky, and brought them to the man to see what he would call them; and whatever the man called a living creature, that was its name. The man gave names to all the cattle, and to the birds of the sky, and to every beast of the field, but for Adam there was not found a helper suitable for him.

So the Lord God caused a deep sleep to fall upon the man, and he slept; then He took one of his ribs and closed up the flesh at that place. The Lord God fashioned into a woman the rib which He had taken from the man, and brought her to the man.

The man said, "This is now bone of my bones, and flesh of my flesh; she shall be called Woman, because she was taken out of Man." For this reason a man shall leave his father and his mother, and be joined to his wife; and they shall become one flesh.

This is the creation account of man and woman being made as partners suitable for one other—natural complements. He could have made two Adams and two Eves; He could have done whatever He wanted, but He chose, in His wisdom, to make man and woman as separate complements.

- Genesis 19:1-13

Now the two angels came to Sodom in the evening as Lot was sitting in the gate of Sodom. When Lot saw them, he rose to meet them and bowed down with his face to the ground.

And he said, "Now behold, my lords, please turn aside into your servant's house, and spend the night, and wash your feet; then you may rise early and go on your way." They said however, "No, but we shall spend the night in the square." Yet he urged them strongly, so they turned aside to him and entered his house; and he prepared a feast for them, and baked unleavened bread, and they ate.

Before they lay down, the men of the city, the men of Sodom, surrounded the house, both young and old, all the people from every quarter; and they called to Lot and said to him, "Where are the men who came to you tonight?

Bring them out to us that we may have relations with them." But Lot went out to them at the doorway, and shut the door behind him, and said, "Please, my brothers, do not act wickedly. Now behold, I have two daughters who have not had relations with man; please let me bring them out to you, and do to them whatever you like; only do nothing to these men, inasmuch as they have come under the shelter of my roof."

But they said, "Stand aside." Furthermore, they said, "This one came in as an alien, and already he is acting like a judge; now we will treat you worse than them." So they pressed hard against Lot and came near to break the door. But the men reached out their hands and brought Lot into the house with them, and shut the door. They struck the men who were at the doorway of the house with blindness, both small and great, so that they wearied themselves trying to find the doorway.

Then the two men said to Lot, "Whom else have you here? A son-in-law, and your sons, and your daughters, and whomever you have in the city, bring them out of the place; for we are about to destroy this place, because their outcry has become so great before the Lord that the Lord has sent us to destroy it."

This passage makes clear that God takes the sin of sexual perversion—that is, the changing of His divine order and plan—very seriously. The Sodomites were irredeemable in their yielding to their own sin of homosexuality.

We must understand that all humans have areas of sin weakness. This is to remind us of our need for Jesus' forgiveness and for our depending on Him for strength and purity in our daily lives, not as an excuse to give in to our sins. For some, our weak area could be anger, pornography, alcohol, drugs, unfaithfulness, control, love for money/acquiring stuff, homosexuality, fear, etc.

Lot, in his fear for the safety of his guests, chose to compound his own sin of compromise by offering the men of the city his own virgin daughters in order to protect his guests. Yielding to our sin will usually lead us to more sin and the possible destruction of our lives and the lives of those we love. Desperation in one's sin is never an excuse to yield to more sin.

- Leviticus 18:22

You shall not lie with a male as one lies with a female; it is an abomination.

This is a clear command from God to avoid homosexuality.

- Leviticus 20:13

If there is a man who lies with a male as those who lie with a woman, both of them have committed a detestable act; they shall surely be put to death. Their bloodguiltiness is upon them.

Here is an even clearer warning not to go against God's plan for man and woman. This verse is in a passage dealing with a variety of sexual sins along with the sacrificing/killing of infants. All the sins listed here cause destruction and ruined lives of people, families, and society. God takes such destruction very seriously, as this passage conveys.

God demands us to pursue holiness, because the opposite is destructive to us and to society. God loves us, but He hates sin—it destroys what He formed and fashioned us to be (Psalm 139:13-14). We need never to take sin lightly.

Even though homosexuality is never God's plan for us, God's way is always forgiveness. The only unforgiveable sin is the rejection of Jesus as Lord and Savior. Hebrews 10:10-12 and 10:17-18 look at God's grace toward us. Even though sin, if pursued, will kill what we could have been, the gift of Jesus to us is forgiveness (Romans 6:23).

Homosexuality is destructive to lives and families, but God's grace, through Jesus, is enough to cleanse all sins when one comes to Him. But when sin is pursued, destruction is the result.

- Romans 1:18-32

For the wrath of God is revealed from heaven against all ungodliness and unrighteousness of men who suppress the truth in unrighteousness, because that which is known about God is evident within them; for God made it evident to them. For since the creation of the world His invisible attributes, His eternal power and divine nature, have been clearly seen, being understood through what has been made, so that they are without excuse. For even though they knew God, they did not honor Him as God or give thanks, but they became futile in their speculations, and their foolish heart was darkened. Professing to be wise, they became fools, and exchanged the glory of the incorruptible God for an image in the form of corruptible man and of birds and four-footed animals and crawling creatures.

Therefore God gave them over in the lusts of their hearts to impurity, so that their bodies would be dishonored among them. For they exchanged the truth of God for a lie, and worshiped and served the creature rather than the Creator, who is blessed forever. Amen.

For this reason God gave them over to degrading passions; for their women exchanged the natural function for that which is unnatural, and in the same way also the men abandoned the natural function of the woman and burned in their desire toward one another, men with men committing indecent acts and receiving in their own persons the due penalty of their error.

And just as they did not see fit to acknowledge God any longer, God gave them over to a depraved mind, to do those things which are not proper, being filled with all unrighteousness, wickedness, greed, evil; full of envy, murder, strife, deceit, malice; they are gossips, slanderers, haters of God, insolent, arrogant, boastful, inventors of evil, disobedient to parents, without understanding, untrustworthy, unloving, unmerciful; and although they know the ordinance of God, that those who practice such things are worthy of death, they not only do the same, but also give hearty approval to those who practice them.

This is yet another very clear passage indicating that people choose to yield to the homosexual lifestyle—that is, they were not born into it.

- 1 Corinthians 6:9-11

Or do you not know that the unrighteous will not inherit the kingdom of God? Do not be deceived; neither fornicators, nor idolaters, nor adulterers, nor effeminate, nor homosexuals, nor thieves, nor the covetous, nor drunkards, nor revilers, nor swindlers, will inherit the kingdom of God. Such were some of you; but you were washed, but you were sanctified, but you were justified in the name of the Lord Jesus Christ and in the Spirit of our God.

God's words through Paul confirm that homosexuality is a sin with dire consequences. Yet, this sin is included among other sins that many have committed—"such were some of you"—that were forgiven and cleansed through a relationship of surrender to Jesus Christ. In other words, there is forgiveness for AND freedom from the sin of homosexuality! This is a beautiful passage.

- 1 Timothy 1:8-11

But we know that the Law is good, if one uses it lawfully, realizing the fact that law is not made for a righteous person, but for those who are lawless and rebellious, for the ungodly and sinners, for the unholy and profane, for those who kill their fathers or mothers, for murderers and immoral men and homosexuals and kidnappers and liars and perjurers, and whatever else is contrary to sound teaching, according to the glorious gospel of the blessed God, with which I have been entrusted.

Here we see again that, in Jesus, there is both forgiveness for and freedom from homosexuality.

4. If the struggling child is a Christian…

… then the basic questions are not about gender confusion or homosexuality. Rather, the questions are, "Do I want to walk with Jesus? Do I really trust His plan for my life and for how He made me more than I trust my feelings (Proverbs 3:5-6)? Do I love and fear Him enough to follow Him (1 Corinthians 10:31)? What do I trust—my emotions or the God of the universe who formed me in my mother's womb (Psalm 139:13-16)?"

5. Practical helps for parents
- Continue to pray for God to strengthen and bring your child back to Him, no matter what He has to do. He knows your heart and love for your child. God loves your child deeply also, and He gave His only son, Jesus, for your child.
- Remember that repenting of homosexuality is difficult, just like repenting of other sexual sins like pornography, etc. Be patient as your child struggles, but stand your ground regarding the truth that Jesus is the only freedom your child needs. Continue to love and be patient for God to work in him.
- Build relationships with a support group of other parents traveling the same difficult path as you.
- Do not condemn. That is God's job only. He loves your child as much as you and wants them to find forgiveness and freedom just like He did for you.
- Share truth to them with love and a broken heart.

- Remember, the main issue is to know and follow Jesus (see Matthew 22:37-40; 2 Corinthians 5:17).
- What if you don't handle the situation well? What if you lose your temper and blow it? Read 1 John 1:9.
- Know sources of support. Gather prayer support from other believers.
- Realize there is no "gay gene." It is a lifestyle choice! There is no simple, biological, genetic pathway to homosexuality.

Conclusion

Welcome to the journey, dear parent. It will not be easy, but our Lord, Savior, and King—Jesus—will walk with you through this valley, as He will through all of your life (Psalm 23). He will be sufficient for this time. Use this difficult season of your life to delve deeper into your walk with Jesus and into His Word. He is sufficient!

Finally, remember: the Bible condemns homosexual behavior, NOT homosexual people.

For further reading

Robert Gagnon. *The Bible and Homosexual Practice: Texts and Hermeneutics*. Nashville, TN: Abingdon Press, 2001.

Pam Gibbs. *Designed by God: Answers to Students' Questions about Homosexuality*. Nashville, TN: Lifeway Press, 2004.

Don Schmierer. *An Ounce of Prevention: Preventing the Homosexual Condition in Today's Youth*. Santa Ana, CA: Promise Publishing, 2002.

CHAPTER 11

RAISING CHILDREN IN A CROSS-CULTURAL CONTEXT

By Robin Covington

Twenty-five years ago, we packed small pieces of our lives into 22 assorted pieces of luggage and footlockers. I wondered how moving to Russia would impact my children. Would they grow up and write a tell-all exposé about the heartless parents who forced them to grow up in a new culture? Would I be the villain in the book?

Friends and acquaintances were not much help during this process. The first question they would ask upon hearing our plans to move overseas was, "Are you taking your kids?"

Of course, that question sent my world into a tailspin. What did people think we were going to do with our children? Leave them with grandparents, or put them in an orphanage? I wondered if we were crazy for taking our kids out of their comfortable American life and culture.

My husband and I had to stop in the middle of this craziness, draw a deep breath, and then look to God for guidance. God had called and directed us to make this move, as a family, and we had to trust in His provision.

And God was faithful. Every step of the way.

I have watched many expat families come and go while living overseas. Some made good transitions; others did not. The one thing we all had in common: learning to live in another culture was difficult.

The makeup and personality of every family is different. What works for one family may not work for another. However, there are several lessons I have learned over the years that I believe can help all parents raising children in a cross-cultural context.

Upon arrival in our new country, my biggest shock was discovering that many things I did as a parent did not change. I still had to feed, clothe, and provide for my children's physical needs. I bandaged their boo-boos, kissed away their tears, and celebrated their joys. We continued to teach our children about spiritual matters using Deuteronomy 6:6-7 as a guide. We tried to model for our children how to walk in God's ways.

None of these things changed. However, a few surprises lurked around the corner.

Culture

First, I realized the need to help my children learn to appreciate a new culture. I looked around, overwhelmed by the differences of living in Russia. These people were doing everything wrong! I felt obliged to help them correct the error of their ways.

Wrong! I was the one who was mistaken. My family's new mantra became, "Different is not wrong, just different." Yes, we preferred our pancakes thick and fluffy, but were thin crepes wrong or just different? Was mayonnaise on pizza wrong or just different? (I was pretty sure mayonnaise on pizza would always be a mistake, but I came to accept it as just different.)

I remember reading the story in Acts 10 where God shows Peter in a dream that it is okay to eat food traditionally labeled unclean. I could relate to Peter's startled statement, "By no means, Lord, for I have never eaten anything unholy and unclean" (Acts 10:14). As I balked against change, I am sure God chuckled.

Our family began learning to eat and live differently, and we survived to tell about it. One of the first food lessons I learned involved garlic.

Garlic is the Russian cure-all. When flu season kicks in, all Russians double or triple their garlic intake. For the best results, it must be raw. You can eat a whole clove by itself, enthrone it upon a piece of bread, or chop it up and add it to your salad.

If you are a preschooler, your mother will talk you into wearing a cute new necklace. It involves string, a small plastic egg with holes punched in it, and a clove of garlic. The first time I walked into a preschool during flu season, I wondered if there had been a vampire outbreak and I was the only one not protected by the Garlic Force.

Convinced this garlic obsession was nonsense, I decided to do some research. I discovered that raw garlic has antibacterial, anti-fungal, and even anti-parasitic properties. If you rub fresh garlic all over yourself, it will get rid of fleas and ticks. Of course, parasites are not the only ones who will flee from your garlicky presence.

That is how I discovered the traditional "Russian antibiotic" of raw garlic had documented healing properties. What I thought was wrong, was merely different. I must confess, I never made my kids wear garlic necklaces, but we did learn to up our garlic intake during flu season.

We purposefully jumped into the local culture and life. We celebrated Russian holidays, ate strange foods, learned about favorite actors and singers. Disco may have died in America, but it was alive and flourishing in Eastern Europe.

The first time we returned to America to visit family, my mom remarked that my kids ate the weirdest foods. She did not know the battles we had fought over food. Our children learned to eat, without complaint, the food offered in a Russian home. Fortunately, copious amounts of bread graced every Russian table. Our kids learned they could push any unappetizing food down their throat with a piece of bread. Being helpful parents, we discretely demonstrated the technique of pushing the food around your plate so it looked like we had eaten some but were too full to finish.

Of course, there are always elements in any culture that you need to be aware of and discuss with your children. Many things are fun and exciting, but there are also things that may be morally wrong. We had to help our kids navigate these areas in a cross-cultural setting.

I often prayed that my son and daughter would learn to love the people and culture of our host country. Later, when our daughter, Corrie, was in college, she brought a volunteer team of students to Russia during spring break. After this trip, Corrie called us and commented that she realized she did not return to Russia just because her parents lived there. She returned because she deeply loved Russia and the Russian people. God had heard my prayers.

Language

Learning the local language was vital to my children's adjustment. We all shed many tears in the process. In the long-term, the rewards were worth the pain. My kids were able to make friends in our neighborhood and feel comfortable in the culture. Often, they were mistaken for being native Russian speakers. That is one of the advantages of learning a second language as a child. No one ever mistook my accent as a Russian accent. It may have been the Texas drawl that gave me away.

An unexpected advantage of our kids learning the local language was that we gained two translators. For free! They learned the language much faster than we did. One day, as our family strolled along the road, an elderly man leaned out a nearby window and yelled at us in Russian. My husband and I exchanged glances and wondered aloud what the man said. Our teenage son piped up and informed us that we really did not want to know what the man said. It gave me pause, as I wondered where our son picked up this knowledge of curse words.

Another cringe-worthy language moment occurred when our daughter innocently blurted out a curse word at church. The entire congregation hushed and stared at her in horror. She was repeating a word she had heard a friend say, but she did not fully realize its meaning. Yes, there were times we had to pull out the dictionary and have a discussion about the appropriateness of certain words, but for the most part, learning the language was a huge benefit to living cross-culturally.

Without the local language, children end up isolated, restricted to playing alone or only with their brothers and sisters. They are often afraid of the unknown. I saw this fear reflected in our daughter the first year of our overseas experience. Corrie was always the bubbly extrovert of our family, but she became quiet and withdrawn during that time. She feared being separated from us or getting lost while riding public transportation. We talked with both of our children and set up an emergency plan in case of separation on the subway or bus. It took time, but once Corrie became more proficient in her language abilities, the fear of public transportation began to recede. She needed to feel confident in her ability to talk and explain herself to locals. This process did not happen overnight. It was well over a year before our daughter reverted to her normal bubbly personality.

Often, we met expats whose families never learned the language of their host culture. They lived in an "American" bubble, protected from the culture around them. Their children missed the incredible opportunity to appreciate the beauty and richness of the host culture.

Education

For families with children, education is always a concern when living in a cross-cultural context. Educational opportunities vary widely from country to country. Options may include national schools, private English-speaking schools, home-schooling, and boarding schools.

When we arrived in Russia, Adam was 12 years old, and Corrie was 8. Most of our colleagues had preschool-aged children, and no one had experience with national school. I knew that, since Adam was a pre-teen, the national school would be a difficult adjustment for him. After much prayer, I decided to home-school our kids.

I was terrified. I had absolutely no background in home-schooling. I struggled with a math deficiency, as did my husband. My children were doomed to flunk algebra if I was their teacher. I convinced myself that they would not be accepted by any college because they lacked a high school diploma.

Fortunately, I found a "How to Homeschool for Dummies" manual, and, with much trepidation, I began teaching my children. I discovered that my kids were good students, and I was a very impatient teacher. I am ashamed to confess that when Corrie struggled with chemistry, I told her I did not care what her final grade was, as long as she passed. (Yes, I also had a chemistry deficiency.) After many prayers, both of my children managed to graduate from high school and go on to college.

As I observed colleagues raising children in a cross-cultural context, I quickly realized there is not a one-size-fits-all answer to educational concerns. Personally, I believe that national school is the best option, particularly if you want your children to be comfortable in the local culture. In spite of that opinion, I chose to home-school my kids because of their ages.

As a parent, it is important to keep an open mind as you research the options in your area. Talk to other parents about their experiences. Do not immediately rule out options such as boarding school for high-schoolers, or attending national school and supplementing with home school for a few subjects. Explore the possibilities, then take your findings to the Lord. Pray for wisdom to know what is best for your child, then follow God's direction. During the years of home-schooling, my daily verse was, "I can do all things through Him who strengthens me" (Philippians 4:13).

National Church

When we began attending church in our new culture, a whole new teaching opportunity reared its head. The first time we participated in the Lord's Supper, I remember my children's horror as they witnessed everyone drinking from a common cup rather than using individual cups. Of course, the kids did not realize how shocked the adults were when we discovered the grape juice was wine.

It seems there were many new rules to learn at church—"do not pray with your hands in your pockets"; "never lay your Bible on the floor"; "do not tell jokes or laugh too loud in church"; "always stand or kneel during prayers"; "married women should wear scarves on their heads."

Then there was the custom of greeting everyone with a "holy kiss" at the end of the church service. You were not allowed to kiss everyone; women kissed women and shook hands with men, and vice versa. I often kidded Adam that his first kiss was from Igor, his Russian Sunday School teacher.

We had to help our children learn to differentiate between American Christian culture, Russian Christian culture, and biblical culture. Even as an adult, I realized that many of the things I assumed to be biblical practices were only church traditions. We had to teach our children to examine all practices through the lens of Scripture, using 2 Timothy 3:16 as a guide: "All Scripture is inspired by God and profitable for teaching, for reproof, for correction, for training in righteousness."

As we worshiped alongside the local body of believers, something unexpected happened. The blinders of tradition fell from our eyes. With our newly opened eyes, we realized that many things we believed to be important were no more than wood, hay, or straw (1 Corinthians 3:12-15). Was it important if we all drank from one common cup or individual cups? No. What was important was the fact that we were celebrating the ordinance of the Lord's Supper with fellow believers. We helped our children realize that even though we did not agree with all the local traditions, we could respect them as long as they did not violate Scriptural teachings.

Self-Identity

One of the hardest questions for my children to answer was, "Where is home?" They struggled with the answer. Is home the city where they were born, their passport country, or the place where they currently reside?

As an adult who lived the majority of my life in America, I did not struggle with this question. I loved America and her culture, and my roots ran deep. It was hard to accept that my children did not share these same feelings.

When Adam and Corrie returned to America to begin college, this point hit home. They were not necessarily happy to be back in America. Of course, some of the conveniences and food were enjoyable, but my children did not view American culture through the same lens I did. They saw excess, rampant materialism, and the shallowness of many of their peers who were more concerned with their appearance than with the needs of others.

The American church was also a shock. Our kids were used to small churches or home groups. I remember visiting a large church on our first Sunday back in America. My children's jaws dropped as the pastor talked about raising $2 million to build a gym. They looked at me in disbelief and questioned why the church was using the money for itself instead of giving it to help others.

In some ways, it hurt my feelings that my children did not understand the specialness of America. I had tried to keep them in touch with American culture by celebrating American holidays like Fourth of July and Thanksgiving while we were living overseas. But I realized that growing up in another culture had broadened their worldview, and they saw things differently than I did. Maybe, they saw things more clearly.

I ran across a poem that helped my understanding of my kids' struggles. It was written by a TCK (Third Culture Kid) and expresses vividly the struggles of a TCK living between two cultures.

"Colors"

I grew up in Yellow Country.
But my parents are Blue.
I'm Blue.
Or at least, that is what they told me.

But I play with the Yellows.
I went to school with the Yellows.
I spoke the Yellow language.
I even dressed and appeared to be Yellow.

Then I moved to the Blue land.
Now I go to school with the Blues.
I speak the Blue language.
I even dress and look Blue.

But deep down inside me,
something's Yellow.
I love the Blue country,
but my ways are tinted with Yellow.

When I am in Blue land,
I want to be Yellow.
When I am in Yellow land,
I want to be Blue.

Why can't I be both?
A place where I can be me.
A place where I can be green.
I just want to be green.[159]

---

[159]By Whitni Thomas, TCK (1991).

As parents of TCKs, we have to help our children walk this road between two cultures, to help them blend the blue and yellow to form their personal shade of green.

We must help our children understand that, as Christians, we are all foreigners living in a place that is not our home. "For our citizenship is in heaven, from which also we eagerly wait for a Savior, the Lord Jesus Christ" (Philippians 3:20). We are sojourners whom God placed on this earth, striving to live well in a place where we do not feel comfortable and looking forward to the day we will be at home with God.

Death of Dreams

Raising children overseas resulted in the death of some of *my* favorite dreams for my kids—dreams of being with extended family for milestones in their lives such as births, graduations, engagements, weddings, deaths. Funny, I found the dreams for my children were the hardest ones to release. I was willing to give up those things for myself, but not for my kids.

I found myself trying to make up for what I imagined Adam and Corrie were missing. I wanted to be sure they had what their friends in America had—fancy bicycles, the newest electronic gadget, stylish clothes. I asked family and friends to mail packages of favorite American snack foods like macaroni and cheese, licorice, Doritos, and Reese's Peanut Butter cups. I must confess, the licorice was for me.

Eventually, I realized my children were not suffering due to an inability to eat at McDonald's, attend prom, or wear the latest fashions. As a matter of fact, they were embarrassed when they realized their Russian friends did not have more than one or two sets of clothes, while they had a closet full of outfits. Of course, there were times we treated ourselves to something special, but as a general rule, our family learned to live with what we could find locally. We tried to model for our children the example of Paul found in Philippians 4:12—"I know what it is to be in need, and

I know what it is to have plenty. I have learned the secret of being content in any and every situation, whether well-fed or hungry, whether living in plenty or in want" (NIV).

I recognized that if my husband and I were happy, generally the kids would follow our lead. If we were always moaning and complaining about things, the kids would do the same.

I knew a family that adopted a "one complaint a day" policy. You were only allowed one daily complaint about the local culture. Of course, it is appropriate to acknowledge that things are hard and let our children express their emotions. There is a time to shed tears and a time to laugh. We all have good and bad days. But sometimes we need a shift in focus.

I had to shift my focus from *my* dreams for my children, to what God wanted for them—to recognize the blessings He daily showered upon them. I claimed the promise of Jeremiah 29:11 for my children—"'For I know the plans I have for you,' declares the Lord, 'plans to prosper you and not to harm you, plans to give you hope and a future'" (NIV). As I laid my dreams for my children at the feet of Jesus, His comfort fell like healing rain on my soul.

Loss of Relationships

The loss of relationships is one of the biggest difficulties children face when living overseas. They are always saying goodbye to someone. First, we left America, and our children had to say farewells to grandparents, aunts, uncles, cousins, and friends. Then they made friends with other kids from missionary or embassy families, and suddenly there would be a turnover, and they would say goodbye to those friends. When we moved to another town, saying goodbye to national friends was excruciating. Our children realized there was a possibility they would never see these precious friends again.

Fortunately, technological advances make it easier to keep in touch with friends and family around the world. As internet capabilities improved, our children were able to maintain relationships around the globe. Adam met a girl at a conference in a neighboring country, and they corresponded by email for a couple of years. They saw each other once a year, maybe twice. Personally, I liked the long-distance relationships. I did not have to worry about enforcing curfews and, practically speaking, email made for a cheap date. Breaking up by email was not quite as earth-shattering as having it happen in person.

I struggled with how to help my children say goodbye. I never found an antidote for their pain. I let them know it was okay to mourn lost relationships. Tears show that we loved, and loving is important. David cried out to God in his pain, saying, "You keep track of all my sorrows. You have collected all my tears in your bottle. You have recorded each one in your book" (Psalm 56:8, NLT). I reminded my children that God understands their pain, and He brings comfort. I prayed that God would keep their hearts tender and open to making new relationships.

Spiritual Gifts

As my kids matured, I prayed that they would each discover their spiritual gifts and find a way to use them in our new culture. Whether we lived in America or another country, I felt this was vital to their spiritual growth. Of course, we were serving as missionaries, and our children participated in our activities and outreach plans. I felt it was important that they found a way to minister using their particular spiritual gifts as outlined in 1 Peter 4:10—"As each one has received a special gift, employ it in serving one another as good stewards of the manifold grace of God."

Our son was a typical teenager. He loved music and played the guitar. I always joked that I could tell how the day was going to progress by the type of music I heard coming from Adam's room each morning. If it was heavy metal, I knew it was going to be a rough day. When the music was a little mellower, maybe soft rock, the day would be smoother.

We had good friends who fed Adam's love of music by providing him with the newest CDs. He shared these CDs with Sasha, his guitar teacher. Sasha played in a Russian rock band and enjoyed learning new music. When Sasha returned the CDs, he would comment that he had translated the songs and realized the songs spoke of Jesus. Sasha's questions gave Adam the perfect opportunity to talk about spiritual matters.

As a result, Adam had the chance to host a 30-minute radio show on a local Christian station in Russia. This small station received lots of CDs of Christian music from America, but they did not know anything about the singers. So Adam and another American friend were asked to introduce the new music and tell about the singers. The broadcast was called "Rock for Jesus."

Truthfully, we were excited about this opportunity, though a little apprehensive. We were working with the Russian Baptist Union, and they were very conservative. When the *babushkas* (grandmothers) heard this music on their radio station, they called it "devil music." But the college students loved it.

I never dreamed that my 15-year-old son would host a radio show in Russia. It was a gift from God and may have contributed to Adam's decision to pursue a degree in communications.

The End of the Story

Well, my kids are all grown-up now. They are both married and have blessed us with amazing grandchildren. I have to say ... my kids are practically normal.

There are a few eccentricities that pop up from time to time. My kids may not recognize the musical hits that most of their American peers know, but they can sing along with every Jim Croce, John Denver, Wayne Watson, and Sandi Patti song you play. (iTunes did not exist during their childhood, and updating our tunes was not easy.)

They also do not recognize jokes about popular American TV shows. We relied on my mom to send VHS tapes of American shows, and her tastes ran to "Dr. Quinn" and "Little House on the Prairie." Fortunately, the guy upstairs had a complete set of "Star Trek: Voyager" tapes, so we were able to expand their horizons and "boldly go where no man has gone before."

Sometimes, this gap in their knowledge of American culture may be a little embarrassing. But in most cases, they have learned to cover it well. Fortunately, they learned much more valuable lessons during their years overseas.

My kids learned to love and appreciate other cultures. For them, comfort food is as likely to be a bowl of borscht as an American hamburger. They learned a new language, and to this day, they are drawn to the refugee and the immigrant.

They discovered that there are more important things than wearing brand-name sneakers and jeans. Relationships are more important than time or money. My kids saw poverty and suffering and learned to discern the difference between want and need.

Our children learned that love could cross all cultures and barriers. They saw God's miracles on a daily basis as He transformed lives, provided protection, and lavished love upon our family.

In many ways, my children became global nomads. They know how to navigate busy international airports, respond to customs agents, handle different currencies, ride public transportation, and realize the importance of always having their passport in hand. Corrie and her family currently live and work overseas. Adam travels abroad several times a year as part of his job as a videographer. They love experiencing new cultures.

As parents shepherding children in a cross-cultural setting, we made many mistakes. We were floundering in a new culture and language, trying to keep our heads above water. We watched our children struggle through difficult circumstances. We turned to God and watched in amazement as He used these same circumstances to mold our children into the adults they are today. We simply had to place our kids in His hands.

For our family, the blessings of a cross-cultural life far outweighed the sacrifices.

CHAPTER 12

DEALING WITH THE LOSS OF A CHILD

By Matt Miller

Humanity has an innate desire to beat the odds. When the Powerball Lottery jackpot tops the multi-hundred-million-dollar mark, folks line up around the block to buy a ticket even though the odds of winning are less than one in 292 million. As March approaches and the NCAA tournament bracket seeds are announced, the office copier works overtime for folks trying to fill out their "perfect" bracket, despite the fact that the odds of filling out a perfect bracket are one in 9,223,372,036,854,777,808 (yes, that's quintillion for the mathematically challenged among us).

The odds of a thoroughbred winning the Kentucky Derby are nearly one in 25,000, and on that first Saturday in May, when 20 horses race around Churchill Downs' 1.25-mile track, it is referred to as "the greatest two minutes in sports." Why? Because everyone wants to beat the odds … and beating the odds at the derby can be profitable.

According to the most recent National Institutes of Health data, in the U.S., one out of every 709 pregnancies ends with a child being carried to full-term only to die before or during labor. Danna Joy Miller, our daughter, is part of that fractional percentage.

On November 2, 2011, we beat the odds. This was the day of the greatest defeat of our lives.

Danna was our first child. After seven years of marriage, the Lord had blessed us with a pregnancy. As new-parents-to-be, we were nervous. We were excited. We were optimistic. We thought we were prepared.

We had done the gender reveal party, the baby showers, and the prenatal classes. We stocked up on diapers and wipes, we had painted the nursery in an Etsy-approved color, and we knew the arguments from both sides of the "Do we vaccinate?" debate.

We had gone to classes on how to install a car seat, and even though we were rookies, we had done our homework about birthing plans, epidurals, and even lactation. We had picked out a name, being ever so careful that it wouldn't rhyme with anything obscene or have the ability to be morphed into an object of torment for our daughter for years to come. We thought we had planned for it all.

We had not. The one thing we hadn't prepared for was saying goodbye to our little girl.

The day started normally enough. I had been up late the night before putting a finish coat on a dresser that I was building for the nursery. Natalie had done a few loads of laundry—baby clothes— and it was remarkable how many outfits you could fit into one load of wash when they were so tiny. The countdown clock was ticking, and we were excitedly awaiting becoming parents. Our regularly scheduled 40-week OB appointment was later that morning; we said our goodbyes and planned to rendezvous at our doctor's office in a few hours.

It was in that office that all of our planning began to fail. I'll never forget the words, "We're having trouble finding a heartbeat." They were delivered not with the normal, optimistically upbeat tone of our obstetrician but with a very clinical "I am a doctor and there is now a problem to solve" tenor. We were immediately taken into emergency Labor and Delivery, where an ultrasound confirmed our worst fears: Danna, our daughter, had left this world before she had even entered it.

What happened next is a bit fuzzy, as if time stood still, yet as if it was all over in an instant. Our dream had become a nightmare, and this nightmare was our reality. There were doctors and nurses and a support team. Natalie labored for hours to deliver our daughter. We held our lifeless newborn, we cried—a lot—and we said goodbye.

After delivering our daughter, there was pain, both physically and emotionally. Sometime after delivery, and after our goodbyes, the baby identification RFID tags we were wearing were cut from our wrists, and we were escorted from the birthing suite to a room far away from the maternity ward for postnatal recovery. Natalie hurt. I hurt. There were more questions than answers, and our daughter was gone.

Life had a completely numb feeling about it. Natalie and I had both experienced loss before, but they were losses of loved ones who had lived life. The losses that we had experienced before were losses of memories, shared experiences, and time together; what we lost with Danna was potential.

We would never meet, and maybe intimidate, Danna's first boyfriend. We would never teach her to ride a bike or drive a five-speed transmission. We would never have daddy/daughter time together. I would never walk her down the aisle.

There wouldn't be Mommy bandaging scraped knees or binding up a broken heart. There wouldn't be a chance to offer instruction on how to act like a lady or how to navigate college entrance essays. There wouldn't even be dutiful Saturdays spent on the athletic field just knowing our daughter was going to be a pro. There would be none of that.

Instead of leaving the hospital through the front doors with a baby in our arms to experience a future together, we left through a nondescript exit on the second floor of a parking garage to plan a funeral. We left to grieve. However, because of our faith, we were able to grieve with hope. Because of the promises of God, we were able to grieve without the thought that today was the end of our daughter for all eternity.

Around us in the hospital were family and friends. Even before we were able to share our sad news, people began to gather. They came to support us, and some of the greatest support came through

Scripture. Some of the words following are directly from a letter written to us by a friend and mentor.

Danna Joy Miller is Uncondemned in the Presence of Jesus

Natalie and I have confidence that God is sovereign, good, and trustworthy. As Abraham asked in Genesis 18:25, "Shall not the Judge of all the earth deal justly?"

If you, like us, have lost a child, please take comfort in Psalm 107:1, "Oh give thanks to the Lord, for He is good, for His lovingkindness is everlasting." Read, cry, and read again Psalm 23:6—"Surely goodness and lovingkindness will follow me all the days of my life, and I will dwell in the house of the Lord forever"—knowing that God is good.

Know that God loves you and cares for you and wants to comfort you as you grieve:

> The Lord is near to the brokenhearted and saves those who are crushed in spirit. (Psalm 34:18)

> My flesh and my heart may fail, but God is the strength of my heart and my portion forever. (Psalm 73:26)

> He [the Lord] heals the brokenhearted and binds up their wounds. (Psalm 147:3)

> Blessed are those who mourn, for they shall be comforted. (Matthew 5:4)

Find solace in knowing Jesus held children in high regard. Consider His words:

> Truly I say to you, unless you are converted and become like children, you will not enter the kingdom of heaven. Whoever then humbles himself as this

child, he is the greatest in the kingdom of heaven. And whoever receives one such child in My name receives Me; but whoever causes one of these little ones who believe in Me to stumble, it would be better for him to have a heavy millstone hung around his neck, and to be drowned in the depth of the sea. (Matthew 18:3-6)

See that you do not despise one of these little ones, for I say to you that their angels in heaven continually see the face of My Father who is in heaven. (Matthew 18:10)

So it is not the will of your Father who is in heaven that one of these little ones perish. (Matthew 18:14)

Permit the children to come to Me; do not hinder them; for the kingdom of God belongs to such as these. (Mark 10:14)

The Bible indicates a period of safeness for those who have not matured to the point of understanding right from wrong. Romans 1:18-32 indicates that both our consciences and creation itself give proof of the existence of God. Because we suppress the truth, we experience condemnation. Our daughter never suppressed the truth nor did she affirm Adam's sin with her own. She never willfully broke the commands of God. While Jesus is the only way to salvation, Danna never had a willful transgression counted against her, and by that grace of God, she stands now uncondemned in the presence of Jesus.

Your little ones who you said would become a prey, and your sons, who this day have no knowledge of good or evil, shall enter there, and I will give it to them and they shall possess it. (Deuteronomy 1:39)

Following the Israelites' exodus from Egypt, God punished the doubting generation by prohibiting them from entering the promised land. Yet, their children, who had no knowledge of good or evil, did not suffer the same judgment. Because they had no culpability in Israel's sin, the "little ones" were excluded from judgment and allowed to enter the promised land along with Caleb and Joshua.

Although Isaiah 7 certainly communicates a larger teaching (God's faithfulness to a promise made with King David concerning the Davidic dynasty), contained within that passage is neverthe-less an affirmation of an often referred to "age of accountability." Isaiah 7:16 states, "For before the boy will know enough to refuse evil and choose good, the land whose two kings you dread will be forsaken."

Our Daughter Was, and Is, a Person
Created in the Image of God

Despite our loss, we find hope that God knew more about Danna and cared more for Danna than her mother and I can ever imagine. God formed her in the womb, and God knew her days before we even knew she existed.

Danna Joy was made in the image of God. In Genesis 1:26, on the last day of creation, God says, "Let Us make man in Our image, according to Our likeness."

God finished His work with a "personal touch." God formed Adam from the dust and "breathed into his nostrils the breath of life; and man became a living being" (Genesis 2:7).

God created that same *imago dei* in Danna. It is that same breath of life that God gave our baby by sharing His own breath.

> Upon You I was cast from birth; You have been my God from my mother's womb. (Psalm 22:10)

> For You formed my inward parts; You wove me in my mother's womb. I will give thanks to You, for I am fearfully and wonderfully made; wonderful are Your

works, and my soul knows it very well. My frame was not hidden from You, when I was made in secret, and skillfully wrought in the depths of the earth.... (Psalm 139:13-15)

Everyone who is called by My name, and whom I have created for My glory, whom I have formed, even whom I have made.... (Isaiah 43:7)

Before I formed you in the womb I knew you, and before you were born I consecrated you. (Jeremiah 1:5)

But when God, who had set me apart even from my mother's womb and called me through His grace.... (Galatians 1:15)

Not only did God know of the formation of Danna, but He also knew the length of her days. From the womb, our daughter was a person in the eyes of God, and God loved her.

Your eyes have seen my unformed substance; and in Your book were all written the days that were ordained for me, when as yet there was not one of them. (Psalm 139:16)

Natalie and I Know Our Baby is Safe in the Arms of God, and We Will Be Reunited With Her One Day

2 Samuel 12 talks about David's losing a child:

Then his servants said to him, "What is this thing that you have done? While the child was alive, you fasted and wept; but when the child died, you arose and ate food." He said, "While the child was still alive, I fasted and wept; for I said, 'Who knows, the Lord may be gracious to me, that the child may live.' But now he has died; why should I fast? Can I bring him back again? I will go to him, but he will not return to me." (verses 21-23)

What many overlook in trying to determine the meaning of this passage is the completely opposite reaction of David at the death of his other son, Absalom. 2 Samuel 18:33 states,

> The king was deeply moved and went up to the chamber over the gate and wept. And thus he said as he walked, "O my son Absalom, my son, my son Absalom! Would I had died instead of you, O Absalom, my son, my son!"

2 Samuel 19 tells of David's continued mourning for his son. The contrast is obvious. David stopped mourning at the death of the baby; David started mourning at the death of Absalom. Why such a difference? Because David knew that the baby was with Jesus. David was fully confident that he would meet his son in heaven.

People often ask us how we "got over" the death of our daughter, as if losing a child is an illness from which people recover. I bite my cheek and smile, knowing what is meant by their inquisition. Honestly, we are not over it, and I don't know if we ever will be. We assume that what these people are asking is, "What, practically, did you do to move forward after your loss?" We answer their question by sharing that the main thing that has helped us persevere without cracking honestly is God's Word.

Natalie and I have confidence that Danna resides with Jesus. And while we wait for the glorious reunion with our daughter, she lacks for nothing. The God of the universe is providing for her every need.

In some ways, Danna is better off than we are. The book of Job records that he experienced such suffering that he "cursed the day of his birth" (Job 3:1-5, 11, 16-17). Danna has been spared all the hurt, all the sin, and all the suffering that this world contains. The pain that we now feel, and will always feel, our daughter will never know. All she will know is the joy of eternal life and the glorious comfort of our Savior.

Grieving as the Family of God

After our loss, we were surrounded by friends, family, and the church, both locally and globally, who ministered to us. Even while we were in the hospital, a friend stepped up to play traffic cop to coordinate our care and the care of those around us who were also grieving. I know food does not magically appear, nor does housework mysteriously do itself, nor do office responsibilities wondrously handle themselves, but there was nothing that we did other than let our friends minister to us by removing these burdens.

Remaining still and grieving was tough. As a couple who always have the answers and who are always wanting to help others, it was a humbling experience to receive such love. Never have I been more thankful for a church than I was in the days following Danna's passing.

During our mourning, we extended people lots of latitude. When you lose a child, people with the best intentions can say the worst things. We just purposed in our hearts to forgive them.

To the people who told us, "You're young; there will be more," I wanted to shout and become violent, but I understood what they were trying to say; it was just a feeble attempt to grieve with us. We knew there would not be more. If we believe Scripture when it tells us everyone is unique and God knew Danna when she was in the womb, then there will be no other Danna. She was a one-of-a-kind creation, fearfully and wonderfully made; an individual known by God, loved by Him, and created to bring glory to Him. Yes, since our loss, the Lord has blessed us with two beautiful boys, each unique and each individual; but no, there will never be another Danna.

To all the folks who said, "You'll get over this," forgive me for wanting to strangle you while I silently replied, "Bless your heart." The loss of a loved one, regardless of age, is something that you never "get over." Loss is something that you can get *through*, it is something that you can get *beyond*, but it is okay to never get *over* it. Even as I write these words and the emotions well to the surface, it is obvious that the loss of our daughter is not something that we will just get over.

We trusted brothers and sisters who were around us. We had never planned a funeral before. I'm grateful for a pastor who literally took our hands and walked us through what was one of the most trying experiences of our lives.

I never allowed my wife to blame herself. Many times, the irrational comes into play for a woman who loses a child. The most comforting words that Natalie heard from the medical community following the loss of our daughter were, "There was nothing that you could have done." Natalie was diligent in her responsibility as an expectant mother—there were no unpasteurized dairy products, there was no luncheon meat that wasn't cooked thoroughly, there were no high-risk activities that put our daughter's life in jeopardy. No drug use, no alcohol, zero all-night benders. After an autopsy, genetic testing, second looks at our sonograms, and an audit of our medical records, there was no reason found for the loss of our daughter.

We avoided, to some, what seemed like an "easy fix" and turned to God and His Word instead of prescription anti-psychotics, opioids, and anti-depressants. We are grateful not just for fellow believers but for the medical professionals who counseled us that while the latest Rx could certainly numb anything that we were feeling, there was no prescription that could truly take away our hurting.

We are open about our loss. Many people don't want to talk about stillbirths or miscarriages, and we must admit these topics don't make for pleasant dinner conversation. However, there is an appropriate time and place to discuss negative, unhappy, and painful things. We were grateful for those who came beside us and wrapped their arms around us and said, "We've been there."[160]

We accepted that it was okay to be in a spiritually dark place. God is big. And He can handle your doubts. So even as I stood at the funeral next to my baby's casket singing "It Is Well with My Soul," all the while doubting every word, God was big enough to handle my doubt.

Conclusion

Now, more than five years removed from the loss of our daughter, I can truthfully say it is well with my soul. Are we "all better"? No. Will we ever be? On this side of heaven, I doubt it.

Our life has returned to some degree of normal. I can admit that there are now days that go by without any thoughts of Danna or her passing. Each year, as the calendar approaches what was to be Danna's birthday, our house becomes a bit melancholy as we are reminded of our loss. There is still pain and lingering grief from the death of our daughter—not the sharp, earth-shattering kind of pain, but the dull ache of missing a part of us, and the never-to-be-fulfilled longing for the experiences that we will not have with our little girl.

There are still questions Natalie and I are trying to answer. Some are practical questions like, "When and how do we bring up Danna with our two little boys?" And when someone asks, "How many children do you have?"—are we being less than truthful by simply saying we have two little boys instead of getting into a heavy conversation about the loss of a child?

There are also great, big overarching questions like, "Why did we lose our daughter?"

---

[160]See 2 Corinthians 1:3-4: "Blessed be the God and Father of our Lord Jesus Christ, the Father of mercies and God of all comfort, who comforts us in all our affliction so that we will be able to comfort those who are in any affliction with the comfort with which we ourselves are comforted by God."

We're okay having questions; even unanswered questions. There are no hard and fast rules or guidelines to teach us how to handle our mourning.

God may also have some greater purpose behind our loss. We do not know why God took Danna from this world, but in His infinite wisdom and knowledge, could it be that God has some greater purpose?

As Christians who believe life begins at conception, we embrace our daughter's life and celebrate it. There is no need to put a birthday on a tombstone before we are able to celebrate our Creator and the life that He had given. And we know no matter how long the odds seem, in the end, we win: "…and He will wipe away every tear from their eyes; and there will no longer be any death; there will no longer be any mourning, or crying, or pain; the first things have passed away" (Revelation 21:4).

Last Word

By Alex Sibley

After reading this volume, perhaps you are wondering how you can possibly manage the parenting task. That is, how can you handle all the responsibilities, pressures, and challenges associated with rearing children, particularly if things do not go "according to plan," and especially if the ever-elusive payoff of seeing your children walk in righteousness remains only a distant possibility?

How can you endure the unforeseen obstacles that seem to continually and never-endingly crop up? How can you persevere through the sheer exhaustion that comes from raising another human being (or several)? Will it ever be possible to slow down and just enjoy life? More importantly, will it ever be possible to just get some sleep?

And what about the other areas of life? How can you keep the house clean, keep up with finances, and maintain a healthy relationship with your spouse? And most important of all, how can you continue to walk in righteousness yourself and maintain your intimacy with God?

If you have found yourself asking any or all of these questions, there is good news for you: God has called you to this. Children are a gift from the Lord, and so He certainly did not make a mistake when He gave you children. Parenting, then, is a calling—a God-ordained task.

Furthermore, consider Ephesians 2:10, which states, "For we are His workmanship, created in Christ Jesus for good works, which God prepared beforehand so that we would walk in them." Parenting certainly provides many opportunities for "good works." Indeed, every aspect of parenting—even the more unpleasant aspects, such as discipline—is ultimately made up of good works (or at least they are intended to be). Therefore, the things you have to do as a parent were specifically prepared by God for you to do. You were thus appointed by God to be a parent; to handle the responsibilities, pressures, and challenges associated with rearing children.[161] And since God appointed you to do this, He will provide the necessary strength to do it, because that is the kind of God He is—He is faithful.[162]

Finding Strength and Courage

Joshua was charged with leading the nation of Israel into the promised land. He was appointed by God for this task (Deuteronomy 31:23; Joshua 1:6), and God promised to be with Joshua as he strived to accomplish it. "I will be with you," God told him. "I will not fail you or forsake you" (Joshua 1:5b). God later said to him, "Have I not commanded you? Be strong and courageous! Do not tremble or be dismayed, for the Lord your God is with you wherever you go" (Joshua 1:9).

We, too, have been appointed for a task, and what a privilege it is to be entrusted by the Lord with such an important responsibility

---

[161]To say that you are "appointed" for this task is by no means to say that you are alone in it. The point being made is that, as Christians, we all have work prepared by God for us to do; and if you are a parent, that work includes raising your children. But as multiple chapters in this volume indicate, no parent is alone in the rearing of his children—not only does God promise to be with you, but brothers and sisters in Christ should always be willing to come alongside you for mutual support and encouragement.

[162]See, for example, Lamentations 3:22-23: "The Lord's lovingkindnesses indeed never cease, for His compassions never fail. They are new every morning; great is Your faithfulness."

as raising children. Furthermore, because this task has come from God Himself, the words He spoke to Joshua surely apply to us as well. As this volume has hopefully demonstrated, He has commanded us in what we are to do as parents. Therefore, let us be strong and courageous. May we not tremble or be dismayed, for the Lord our God is with us wherever we go and in whatever we do.

For those unfamiliar with Joshua's story, he did succeed in his task; indeed, the Lord was faithful and fulfilled His promise to bring the nation of Israel into the promised land. Joshua's strength and courage—and ultimately, his success—were derived from three tools that he received from God at the beginning of his journey:

1. The assurance of God (Joshua 1:2-5) – God Himself gave Joshua the task, and so Joshua could rest in the fact that he was appointed for it (again, what a privilege).

2. The Word of God (Joshua 1:7-8) – While receiving his initial instruction from God, Joshua was told:

> Be careful to do according to all the law which Moses My servant commanded you; do not turn from it to the right or to the left, so that you may have success wherever you go. This book of the law shall not depart from your mouth, but you shall meditate on it day and night, so that you may be careful to do according to all that is written in it; for then you will make your way prosperous, and then you will have success. (Joshua 1:7b-8)

God commanded meditation on and obedience to His Word, the Bible, in order for Joshua to be prosperous and successful.

3. The presence of God (Joshua 1:5b, 9) – As mentioned above, God assured Joshua that He would never leave him nor forsake him, and how comforting and empowering that thought.

Joshua employed these tools to find eventual success in his task. We have access to those same tools; and while we may not find success as we would define it, if we use those tools, we will know, at the very least, that we have done the will of God to the best of our ability.

So, let us return to the good news shared at the beginning: God has called you to the parenting task. He has prepared the work for you to do. May we not miss how profound that truth is. Furthermore, He has given you the tools to succeed: His assurance, His Word, and His presence. So let us utilize those tools in order to persevere through the hardships and the exhaustion that come from raising children so that we may find success; so that our children may walk in righteousness; so that we may rejoice that our efforts were not in vain.

So as you approach the task of everyday parenting, do not tremble or be dismayed; be strong and courageous!

BIBLIOGRAPHY

Benge, Janet and Geoff Benge. *C.T. Studd: No Retreat*. Seattle, WA: YWAM Publishing, 2005.

Bentley, Vicki. "What does it Cost to Homeschool?" Accessed 1/8, 2017. https://www.hslda.org/earlyyears/Costs.asp.

Blomberg, Craig L. *The New American Commentary: Matthew*. Nashville, TN: Broadman Press, 1992.

Cogan, Michael F. "Exploring Academic Outcomes of Homeschooled Students." *Journal of College Admission* no. 208 (01/01, 2010): 18-25.

Council for American Private Education, "Facts and Studies," Accessed 1/8, 2017.

Criswell, W.A., ed. *The Believer's Study Bible, New King James Version*. Nashville, TN: Thomas Nelson Publishers, 1991.

Dana, H.E. *Lee Rutland Scarborough: A Life of Service*. Nashville, TN: Broadman Press, 1942.

Department of Education, "The Federal Role in Education," Accessed 1/8, 2017. https://www2.ed.gov/about/overview/fed/role.html.

Delitzch, Franz. *Biblical Commentary on the Proverbs of Solomon*. Charleston, SC: BiblioBazaar, 2009.

Dobson, James. *Bringing Up Girls*. Carol Stream, IL: Tyndale House, 2010.

Dunphy, John J. "A Religion for a New Age." *Humanist* 43, no. 1 (Jan, 1983): 23.

Farmer, Brian. "New Public School Policy." *The New American* 29, no. 16 (2013): 24-28.

Farrar, Steve. *King Me*. Chicago, IL: Moody Publishers, 2005.

Fee, Gordon D. *Paul's Letters to the Philippians, New International Commentary on the New Testament*. Grand Rapids, MI: William B. Eerdmans Publishing Co., 1995.

Fernandez, Joaquin and Colin Gunn. *IndoctriNation: Public Schools and the Decline of Christianity in America*, edited by Gunn Productions. Vol. Film 2011.

Fontinelle, Amy. "Paying for K–12 Private School Tuition." MassMutual Financial Group. Accessed 1/8, 2017. https://www.massmutual.com/individuals/educational-articles/paying-for-k-12-private-school-tuition.

Good, Harry Gehman. *A History of American Education*. New York: Macmillan c1962; 2nd ed, 1962.

Graves, Dan. "C.T. Studd Gave Huge Inheritance Away," Christianity.com. n.p., accessed 10/27, 2016. http://www.christianity.com/church/churchhistory/ timeline/1801-1900/c-t-studd-gave-huge-inheritance-away-11630616.html.

Grubb, Norman. *C.T. Studd: Athlete and Pioneer.* Atlantic City, NJ: The World-Wide Revival Prayer Movement, 1947.

Harvard Graduate School of Arts and Sciences Christian Community, "Shield and 'Veritas' History," Accessed 1/8, 2017. http://www.hcs.harvard.edu/~gsascf/shield-and-veritas-history/.

Hildebrandt, Ted. "Proverbs 22:6a: Train up a Child?" *Grace Theological Journal* 9:1 (Spring 1988).

Hodge, Archibald Alexander. *Evangelical Theology: A Course of Popular Lectures.* Carlisle, PA: Banner of Truth Trust, 1990.

Keller, Timothy. *Counterfeit Gods: The Empty Promises of Money, Sex, and Power, and the Only Hope that Matters.* New York: Penguin Books, 2009.

Kena, Grace, William Hussar, Joel McFarland, Cristobal de Brey, Lauren Musu-Gillette, Xiaolei Wang, Jijun Zhang, et al. *The Condition of Education 2016. NCES 2016-144*: National Center for Education Statistics, 2016.

King, Kelly A. "A Comparative Anaylsis of Children's Cognitive and Affective Learning from Selected Bible Story Videos." PhD diss., Southwestern Baptist Theological Seminary, 2009.

Klicka, Chris. "Socialization: Homeschoolers are in the Real World." Home School Legal Defense Association. Accessed 1/8, 2017. http://www.hslda.org/docs/nche/000000/00000068.asp.

Knowles, J.G., James A. Muchmore, and Holly W. Spaulding. "Home Education as an Alternative to Institutionalized Education." *Educational Forum* 58, no. 3 (03/01, 1994): 238-43.

Koehler, Lindsey, Trent Langness, Sarah Pietig, Nicole Stoffel, and Jamie Wyttenbach. *Socialization Skills in Home Schooled Children Versus Conventionally Schooled Children*. LaCrosse, WI: University of Wisconsin, 2002.

Lambert, Heath. *Finally Free: Fight for Purity with the Power of Grace*. Grand Rapids, MI: Zondervan, 2013.

Lewis, Robert. *Raising a Modern-Day Knight: A Father's Role in Guiding His Son to Authentic Manhood*. Carol Stream, IL: Tyndale House Publishers, 1997.

Luther, Martin. *The Christian in Society*, 1. Translated by Jacobs, Charles, edited by Atkinson, J. Philadelphia, PA: Fortress Press, 1966.

MacArthur, John. *Successful Christian Parenting*. Nashville, TN: Word, 1998.

May, Philip R. *Which Way to Educate?* Chicago, IL: Moody Press, American ed., 1975.

Melick, Richard R., Jr. *The New American Commentary: Philippians, Colossians, and Philemon*. Nashville, TN: Broadman Press, 1991.

National Center for Education Statistics, U.S. Department of Education. "Fast Facts – Expenditures," Accessed 1/8, 2017. https://nces.ed.gov/fastfacts/display.asp?id=66.

Nehemiah Institute. "The History of American Education/ Culture," http://www.nehemiahinstitute.com/pdf/TKS-Chart-3.pdf.

Nettles, Tom J. *Teaching Truth, Training Hearts: The Study of Catechisms in Baptist Life.* Amityville, NY: Calvary Press Publishing, 1998.

Newman, Alex. "Common Core: A Scheme to Rewrite Education." *The New American* 29, no. 16 (2013): 10-19.

Oak City Academy, "Homeschool Vs Public School Vs Private School: What's a Parent to do?" Accessed 1/8, 2017. http://oakcityacademy.org/2015/09/29/homeschool-vs-public-school-vs-private-school-whats-a-parent-to-do/.

Office of Non-Public Education, "Statistics about Nonpublic Education in the United States." Accessed 1/8, 2017. https://www2.ed.gov/about/offices/list/oii/nonpublic/statistics.html.

Organization for Economic Co-operation and Development. "Private Schools: Who Benefits." *PISA in Focus* 7, (2011): 1-4.

Osborne, Rick. *Teaching Your Child How to Pray.* Chicago, IL: Moody Press, 2000.

Owens, Waylan. "Preparing a Child's Heart to Respond to Christ." *The Alabama Baptist*, Vol. 175, no. 40 (2010): 9-16.

Parnell, Jessica. "Public, Private, or Home? How to make the Ultimate Decision." Accessed 1/8, 2017. http://www.crosswalk.com/family/homeschool/encouragement/public-private-or-home-how-to-make-the-ultimate-decision.html?p=2.

Potter, Charles Francis and Clara Cook Potter. *Humanism: A New Religion*. New York: Simon and Schuster, 1930.

Phillips, John. *Exploring Proverbs: An Expository Commentary*. Grand Rapids, MI: Kregel Publications, 2002.

Private School Review, "Average Private School Tuition Cost (2016-2017)." Accessed 1/8, 2017. http://www.privateschool-review.com/tuition-stats/private-school-cost-by-state.

Queen, Matt. *Everyday Evangelism*. Fort Worth, TX: Seminary Hill Press, 2015.

Radcliff, James. "Choosing an Education for Your Child: Homeschool vs. Private School." Accessed 1/8, 2017. http://timandolive.com/choosing-an-education-for-your-child-ho-meschool-vs-private-school/.

Ray, Brian. "Research Facts on Homeschooling." National Home Education Research Institute. Accessed 1/8, 2017. http://www.nheri.org/research/research-facts-on-homes-chooling.html.

Ray, Brian D. *Home Educated and Now Adults: Their Community and Civic Involvement, Views about Homeschooling, and Other Traits*. National Home Education Research Institute, 2004.

Redford, Jeremy, Danielle Battle, and Stacey Bielick. *Homes-chooling in the United States: 2012. Statistical Analysis Report. NCES 2016-96*. Washington, D.C.: National Center for Education Statistics, Institute of Education Sciences, U.S. Department of Education, 2016.

Rizzolo, Allison. "Americans View Higher Education as Key to American Dream." Public Agenda. Accessed 1/8,

2017. http://www.publicagenda.org/press-releases/index. php?qid=27.

Rogers, Adrian. *What Every Christian Ought to Know*. Nashville, TN: Broadman and Holman Publishers, 2005.

Samuel, Lawrence R. *The American Dream: A Cultural History*. Syracuse University Press, 2012.

Scarborough, Lee R. *Recruits for World Conquests*. New York: Fleming H. Revell Company, 1914.

Schultz, Glen. *Kingdom Education: God's Plan for Educating Future Generations*. Nashville, TN: LifeWay Press, c2002; Second edition, 2002.

Sizer, Bridget. "Socialization: Tackling Homeschooling's 'S' Word." Accessed 1/8, 2017. http://www.pbs.org/parents/education/homeschooling/socialization-tackling-homeschoolings-s-word/.

Smedley, Thomas. "Socialization of Home Schooled Children: A Communication Approach." Thesis, Master of Science in Corporate and Professional Communication, Radford University, Radford, VA.

Smith, Christian and Melinda Denton. *Soul Searching*. New York: Oxford University Press, 2005.

Smithwick, Dan. *Pillars of the World*. Vol. PowerPoint presentation Nehemiah Institute, 2013.

Spurgeon, C.H. *The Treasury of David*, Vol. 3. McLean, VA: MacDonald Publishing Company, 1990.

Stanton, Glenn and Andrew Hess. "Millennial Faith Participation and Retention," n.p. Focus on the Family, August 2013, accessed 10/21, 2016. http://media.focusonthefamily.com/fotf/pdf/about-us/focus-findings/millenial-faith-retention.pdf#_ga=1.132875596.392784255.1440477650.

Stearns, Richard. *The Hole in Our Gospel.* Nashville, TN: Thomas Nelson, 2009.

Stiles, Gerald. *History of American Education.* Vol. Lecture given at South Carolina Christian school administrators meeting, sponsored by the Association of Christian Schools International (Charleston, SC).

Taylor, Larry. *Running with the Horses: A Parenting Guide for Raising Children to be Servant-Leaders for Christ.* Bloomington, IN: WestBow Press, 2013.

Teach Our History. "The Founding of Education in America." Accessed 1/8, 2017. http://teachourhistory.com/early-education.htm.

Tripp, Tedd. *Shepherding a Child's Heart.* Wapwallopen, PA: Shepherd Press, 2005.

UNICEF Office of Research, "The Convention." Accessed 1/8, 2017. https://www.unicef-irc.org/portfolios/crc.html.

Walker, Jon. "Family Life Council Says It's Time to Bring Family Back to Life." Accessed 1/8, 2017. http://www.sbcannualmeeting.net/sbc02/newsroom/newspage.asp?ID=261.

"Why School? The 48th Annual PDK Poll of the Public's Attitudes Toward the Public Schools." *Phi Delta Kappan* 98, no. 1 (09, 2016): K1-K32.

Widner, Michael and Shane Parker. *TransforMission: Making Disciples through Short-Term Missions*. Nashville, TN: B&H Publishing Group, 2010.

Wuehler, Deborah. "Public, Private, Or Home Education ... what are My Options?" Accessed 1/8, 2017. http://www.crosswalk.com/family/homeschool/getting-started/public-private-or-home-education-what-are-my-options.html.

Zhang, Anlan, Lauren Musu-Gillette, and Barbara A. Oude-kerk. *Indicators of School Crime and Safety: 2015. NCES 2016-079. NCJ 249758*: National Center for Education Statistics, 2016.

Zuck, Roy B. *Precious in His Sight: Childhood and Children in the Bible*. Grand Rapids, MI: Baker Books, 1996.

APPENDIX A

Child's Name	Interests	Life Events to consider	Bible Skills to Target
Everett	Horses/Outdoors	Starting school in the fall/asking quesitons about God/has a new sister	Teach him that the Bible is divided into different books and start learning the names of as many books as he can pronounce
Stories and Scriptures to highlight	Genesis 47 Exodus 14 1 Kings 10:26	1 Thessalonians 5:18 Hebrew 4:12	First five books of both the Old and New Testaments
Stories and Scriptures to highlight			
Stories and Scriptures to highlight			

APPENDIX B

Recommended children's Bibles:

All ages:

HCSB Holman Classic Children's Bible (Holman Bible Publishers, 2013)

The Big Picture Interactive Bible (B&H Kids)

- This is available for different translations. It comes with a free app you and your children can use to hear selected stories.

Specifically for preschoolers:

HCSB Read to Me Bible for Kids (B&H, 2005)

- This has lots of great pictures and includes suggestions for reading selected stories to very young preschoolers.

Specifically for older children:

HCSB Illustrated Study Bible (Holman Bible Publishers, 2013)

Recommended Bible storybooks:

The Big Picture Interactive Bible Storybook (B&H Kids)

- This has 145 illustrated Bible stories from both the Old and New Testaments with a free app like the Interactive Bible. Just be sure to clarify this is a storybook and not the Bible when using this with your children.

The Young Learner's Bible Storybook (by Mary Manz Simon, Standard Publishing, 2002)

- This is not currently widely available in bookstores but can be found easily at Amazon or other online resources. It contains 52 different Bible stories with nice illustrations, which are followed by parent helps, games, and other activities to reinforce the Bible story throughout the week.

Egermeier's Bible Storybook (by Elsie Egermeier, Warner Press Publishers, 2008)

*NOTE: Try to avoid Bibles with gimmicks or added materials such as cartoons or talking toys, etc., as these trivialize the sacred Scriptures.

APPENDIX C

Spurgeon's Catechism for Children[163]:
   1. Who made you?
      A. God.

   2. What else did God make?
      A. God made all things.

   3. Why did God make all things?
      A. For His pleasure.

   4. Why do things work as they do?
      A. Because God made the world.

   5. How do we know about God?
      A. God reveals Himself.

   6. How does God reveal Himself?
      A. In nature and in His Word.

   7. What does God reveal about Himself in nature?
      A. His nature, law, and wrath.

   8. What more does He reveal of Himself in His Word?
      A. God's grace and love for the whole world.

---

[163]Modified by Ed Gravely (Wake Forest, NC: Unpublished, 2008).

9. What is God's Word?
   A. The Bible is God's Word.

10. How many Gods are there?
   A. There is one true God.

11. How many persons are in the Godhead?
   A. Three.

12. Who are these persons?
   A. The Father, Son, and Holy Spirit.

13. Where is God?
   A. He is everywhere.

14. How long has God existed?
   A. He has always been.

15. How is man unique?
   A. He is made in God's image.

16. Who was the first man?
   A. Adam.

17. What was Adam like when God made him?
   A. He was good.

18. Did Adam remain good?
   A. No, he sinned.

19. What is sin?
   A. Disobedience to God.

20. What is the penalty for sin?
   A. Death.

21. What came of Adam's sin?
    A. Death came to all men.

22. How did Adam's sin affect all men?
    A. We all sin like Adam.

23. Must all men die for sin?
    A. No, God has made a way for us to be saved.

24. How may we be saved from sin and death?
    A. Only through Jesus Christ.

25. Who is Jesus Christ?
    A. He is God's Son.

26. Did Jesus ever sin?
    A. No, only He is righteous.

27. What did Jesus do for the whole world?
    A. He took our punishment.

28. How did He do this?
    A. He died, was buried, and then rose again.

29. In addition to death, whom else did Christ conquer?
    A. All His enemies.

30. Are His enemies powerful?
    A. Not compared to Him!

31. What does He do for those who believe in Him?
    A. He declares them righteous.

32. What did He take from His people?
    A. Their sin.

33. How do people receive Christ's forgiveness?
    A. By believing the Gospel and repenting from sin.

34. What is "believing the Gospel"?
    A. Trusting in Christ for salvation.

35. What does the Holy Spirit do for those who believe?
    A. He seals them by His power.

36. How do we recognize true faith?
    A. True faith yields good works.

37. Who are Christ's people?
    A. They are His church.

38. What are the traits of His church?
    A. The Word, church discipline, and the ordinances.

39. What do we do with God's Word at church?
    A. We preach it.

40. How is discipline a trait of His church?
    A. God's people are protected.

41. What are ordinances?
    A. Signs of God's promises.

42. What ordinances are there?
    A. Baptism and the Lord's Supper.

43. Who is head of the church?
    A. Jesus Christ.

44. What offices has Christ appointed in His church?
    A. Pastors and deacons.

45. Is His church perfect?
    A. It is being perfected.

46. When will it be perfect?
    A. At the resurrection.

47. What happens at the resurrection?
    A. Christ judges all men.

48. What of those who are saved?
    A. They dwell with Him forever.

49. What of those who are not saved?
    A. They perish forever.